THE AMAZING LIFE OF

JESUS

History's Great Love Story

GEOFFREY WAUGH

TO MY PARENTS

WHO FIRST CAPTURED MY HEART
WITH THESE STORIES

AND TO OUR CHILDREN AND
OUR CHILDREN'S CHILDREN

AND THEIR CHILDREN WHO LOVE
AND ARE LOVED ALWAYS

Copyright page

© 2024 Geoffrey Waugh

Publisher's Name: Geoffrey Waugh

ISBN: 978-1-962142-45-8

Endorsements

Be enriched. A most helpful telling of the life of Jesus using the biblical text and adding some background and charts. Anyone using this book will be enriched.

Rev Dr John Olley, Research Fellow, Morling College, Australia

Geoff Waugh has written a very helpful devotional book about the Saviour of the world, who is also the loving presence in believers. Having known Geoff for over sixty years, I can testify that every word written proceeds from his own heart of love for Jesus and for all God's children. Geoff has avoided trying to manufacture some theory or a new twist to make the book more colourful. He has used Scripture as his main source and has been faithful to both the divinity and humanity of Jesus as expressed in the Gospels. His use of chronology for headings and the many sub-headings makes the book simpler to absorb, even for an enquirer or new believer. It reminds me a little of Leon Morris's beautiful book The Lord from Heaven. *I warmly commend this book.*

Rev. Dr Tony Cupit, Former Director of the Baptist World Alliance.

This is a very informative, amazing, and powerful book. Thanks to the author for investing hours of research, expressed with his masterful command of language. Alex Johnson

This is a wonderful book and can be read over and over. Thank you, Dr. Waugh. Kerry Rawson

I keep this book with my Bible. It is especially helpful when reading through the Gospels. Cathy Hartwig

The book is beautifully written, and I have learned and understood a lot. I am recommending this book. Kattie Mayson

This book is for those who question Jesus' reality as the Son of God, and for those who search for the details of His amazing life on this earth. Judith Abrey

Impressive! This book is truly outstanding! Congratulations on this remarkable accomplishment. Keep up the exceptional work! Rachael Diaz

Your book cover looks fantastic! Your writing style is exceptional, and I loved how the story unfolded, keeping me captivated. Solomon Emordi

I read your book last night. This is a great book. Thanks for writing this for all of us. Nabeel Sharoon, Pakistan, translator of this book into Urdu, Hindi, Sindhi, Pakistani Punjabi, and Indian Punjabi (renewaljournal.com).

For God so loved the world that he gave his only Son, so that everyone who believes in him may not perish but may have eternal life

JOHN 3:16

We know love by this, that he laid down his life for us and we ought to lay down our lives for one another

1 JOHN 3:16

No one has greater love than this, to lay down one's life for one's friends [Jesus' words on the Jewish day he died.

JOHN 15:13

Contents

PREFACE

Why would such a good man who loved so profoundly and helped so many people be killed? Why did he provoke opposition?

If God walked among us in the person of his Son, why would people want to kill him? Why did so many vehemently oppose him?

That puzzled me as a boy. It still does.

The greatest love story the world has ever seen led to the excruciating death of crucifixion.

Many people have given their lives for other people as soldiers do in war. They die for others, defending their home and country. But Jesus' death was different. God's Son chose to die for us because of his immense love for us. He took our place. His death gives us life. He is the perfect, sinless, eternal sacrifice for us. His blood cleanses us from all our sins as we trust in him. We are forgiven.

But why did so many good people, good religious people, hate him? That puzzled and fascinated me, so I explored that mystery in this book. I wanted to write a summary overview that people of all ages could read.

I always believed in Jesus. Even as a small boy I loved to hear and then read stories about him. He was so unique, so different. I believed his story as a boy and trusted in him. I still do and I hope you do too.

Jesus did what was good. He healed the sick, fed the hungry, set people free from addictions and evil, performed miracles, and even raised dead people. Huge crowds followed him and wanted him to be their king.

Now billions follow him, captivated by his love, the greatest love story of all. You can do that also. I invite you to simply pray something like this: Thank you, Lord, for all you've done. Forgive me for any wrong in my life. I trust in you and give my life to you.

INTRODUCTION

The year on our calendar or diary reminds us of when Jesus was born, approximately. We count the years from his arrival. So when you look at your diary or calendar, you can be reminded again of Jesus.

They called him Yeshua (Joshua/Jesus) of Nazareth, the same name as Moses' famous general who led God's people into their Promised Land. *Yeshua* means "God saves," or "God is salvation."

That name comes to us in English through many translations from **Yeshua** or **Y'shua** in Hebrew and Aramaic, then translated into **Iesous** in Greek, then to **IESVS** in Latin and later as **IESUS** as printed in the first edition of the King James Bible in 1611. Later that century 'J' replaced the 'I' so the English name became **Jesu** (vocative) and **Jesus** (nominative) but eventually as just **Jesus** in English. Other languages have translations such as **Jesu, Yesu,** and **Isa.**

English translations of the Bible used the name *Jesus* for Joshua/Jesus of Nazareth, and the name *Joshua* for others with that same name.[1] So in English the name Jesus became unique and sacred for Jesus of Nazareth, the Son of God, the Saviour of the world. The angel Gabriel announced His name before His birth to both Mary, his mother and to Joseph who married

---

[1] *Iesous* (Yeshua) is translated as Joshua in these verses: Luke 3:29; Acts 7:45; Hebrews 4:8.

3

Mary.[2] Gabriel explained that Yeshua (Joshua/Jesus) had that name because He would save His people from their sins.

The great love story had begun. Jesus came to save us and give us eternal life.

His followers recorded the story of His life and his love in the good news of the four Gospels: Matthew, Mark, Luke, and John. The rest of the New Testament explores the mystery and wonder of that amazing life and love.

Scholars have a bewildering array of theories about the Bible and about who wrote what, and when, and where, and why. I'm content to run with traditional explanations that have been used throughout most of history.

Jesus' unique and wonderful life, his brutal death for us, and his powerful resurrection, all reveal his and God's eternal love for us all. You could pause and thank him right now even as you read this.

John's Gospel emphasizes God's eternal love revealed in Jesus. It includes the most famous passage in the Bible:

> *For God so loved the world that He gave His only begotten Son, that whoever believes in Him should not perish but have everlasting life.*
>
> *For God did not send His Son into the world to condemn the world, but that the world through Him might be saved.*[3]

---

[2] Luke 1:31; Matthew 1:21.

[3] John 3:16-17 (NKJV).

That love, powerfully shown on the cross, has transformed billions of lives, restoring believers to an intimate and eternal relationship with God.

A trinity of three physical metaphors helps me to be constantly aware of, and grateful for, God's presence with us always:

(1) Light surrounds you. By it, you can read this. The sun always shines, even when it's hidden from us. Light shines around us though we may be unaware of it. God is light and in him, there is no darkness at all. We can live in his light.

(2) Blood pumps through your body right now, cleansing and healing. We may be unaware of it until reactions like alarms alert us to our beating heart. Jesus' blood cleanses from all sin, always. We can trust him for he is with us.

(3) We may breathe without being aware of it, or we can be aware and take deep breaths, as you may have done just now! Breath purifies our lungs and body. God is Spirit and like breath or fresh breeze, he can purify us.

May the light of God's love breathe life into you right now.

We've been made in God's image to have an eternal, loving relationship with him that even transcends death. We can know and experience God's unconditional love no matter how far we stray from him. Those who stray most are often the most grateful for his forgiveness and love. We all stray in many ways and we all need forgiveness and we can and should be truly grateful.

God knows and loves us as we are. That makes praying or talking to him easy because he already knows our failures and struggles and welcomes us just as we are. The more honestly we come to him the more he can transform us.

If we have trouble believing we can at least say, "God, if you're there, help me."

Some thoughts may get in the way when we pray or want to talk to God. Just give him those thoughts. He already knows all about it and loves us as we are.

If we reject God's love and mercy by ignoring him and going our own way, we condemn ourselves to eternal darkness away from his light and love.

If we accept his love and forgiveness by believing in him, by trusting him, he gives us life, his eternal life. That makes us new. We are transformed.

Vast numbers of people worldwide of all faiths, and of none, have prayed the prayer in the popular hymn by Charlotte Elliot, 'Just as I am' which includes these adapted verses:

> Just as I am, without one plea
> But that Your blood was shed for me
> And that You bid me come to Thee,
> O Lamb of God, I come, I come.
>
> Just as I am, though tossed about
> With many a conflict, many a doubt,
> Fighting and fears within, without,
> O Lamb of God, I come, I come.

God welcomes us and we can all pray that prayer. A title for Jesus, as in that song, is the sacrificial Lamb of God who takes away our sins.

The Life of Jesus is a vast topic with millions of books written about it. I hope my small contribution gives you a helpful overview. I quote from the New Revised Standard Version unless indicated otherwise, and include many footnotes that you can explore to discover more.

Best of all, of course, are the inspired Gospels now in over 700 different languages in Bible translations and a further 3,500 languages have Bible portions, especially the Gospels. Read and respond to those Gospels.

1 BIRTH AND BOYHOOD

It began at the beginning, this great love story, for "In the beginning, God created the heavens and the earth."[4]

Why did he do that? For us.

He did it for you. He loved you so much that he created you to know and enjoy him now as you read this, and forever. He offers you intimate, infinite love. He created you through the wondrous union of your parents' ecstasy.

He made the earth for us to inhabit, care for, and rule. He made the heavens (plural) for us to inherit, the physical firmament and also the realms of vast, eternal glory prepared especially for us.[5]

He created us free to accept or reject his astounding love. Sadly we went our own way. We all, like sheep, went astray. We all turned to our own way. So God laid on his Servant, his Son, all our iniquity.[6] God saves us through his Son in their great love for us all. You could pause and thank him now as you read this.

In the beginning, Adam and Eve enjoyed an intimate, unashamed relationship with God and each other. Then, like us, they believed lies and went their own way, losing Paradise. But

---

[4] Genesis 1:1.

[5] John 14:1-6; 1 Corinthians 2:9.

[6] Isaiah 53:6. See Isaiah 52:13-53:12, the fourth Servant Song, along with Isaiah 42:1-4; 49:1-6; 50:4-7.

God still blessed and sustained them and their descendants who chose to love him and live for him. Sadly only a few did.

Noah and his family loved and obeyed God and he rescued them from the great flood. People ridiculed him for obeying God and building a huge boat on dry ground – not even in a dry dock. The rainbow became the sign of God's covenant to Noah and his descendants including us.

Abram, a wealthy sheik from the wide fertile Tigris and Euphrates valleys in western Asia, north-east of the Arabian Peninsula (now Iraq), loved and obeyed God. Renamed Abraham (God's friend) he journeyed to the Promised Land, now called Israel from the name given to his grandson who wrestled with an angel or with the Lord.[7] Circumcision became the covenant sign for them and for their descendants through whom God would provide his salvation for us all.

Abraham and his descendants walked that verdant Promised Land, as did Jesus and his followers. So did our family for a month in 1981-82.[8]

King David reigned there for 40 years from around 1000 BC, described as a man after God's own heart who would do what God wanted.[9] That's an amazing picture of God's love and grace for flawed people like David. His descendants ruled from his capital, Jerusalem, till the fall of their kingdom to Babylon. The human Jesus was descended from David through Mary, as was

---

[7] Genesis 17:5; 32:28; 35:9-10.

[8] See *Exploring Israel* in General Books and Biography on renewaljournal.com

[9] 1 Samuel 13:13-14; Acts 13:22

Mary's husband Joseph, also a descendant of the royal line of David.

God blessed his people through history when they remained faithful to him but sadly, like us, they often went their own way, not God's way. The northern kingdom of Israel fell captive to Assyria by 722 BC, as did the southern kingdom of Judah to Babylon from 597 BC. Then Cyrus of Persia allowed the exiles in captivity to return from 538 BC. Babylonian armies took captives in waves of exiles, and the exiles returned in various groups, then speaking Aramaic, a Semitic language similar to their Hebrew Scriptures. Their temple in Jerusalem lay in ruins for 70 years, from 586 BC to 516 BC. The returning exiles became known as Jews, a term derived from the former kingdom of Judah.

Alexander the Great's conquests established Greek culture and language in Israel from around 333 BC, eventually sparking the Maccabean revolt from 165 BC with the Jews gaining independence from 134 BC.

Their independence lasted less than a century till 63 BC when warring brothers appealed to Rome, and Roman armies then invaded and killed 12,000 people, including temple priests, in the siege of Jerusalem. Rome then ruled its province of Judea, also named from the previous kingdom of Judah.

Those searing memories simmered strong in the Israel of Jesus' day when Jews longed for their Messiah to deliver them. Radicals often attacked the Roman occupying armies. Rome retaliated swiftly and brutally. Their armies slaughtered thousands, with hundreds nailed to crosses as in a rebellion led by Judas the Galilean in AD 6 when Jesus was a boy.[10]

Jesus' elderly relatives the old priest Zechariah and his wife Elizabeth lived near Jerusalem, and Zechariah had been literally dumfounded while offering incense in the temple during his roster when the angel Gabriel told him they would have a son to be named John. Zechariah spoke again nine months later at his son's birth when he announced that the boy's name was John.[11]

Six months after that temple encounter, Gabriel appeared again, this time to Mary in the northern hills of Nazareth. He announced that Mary would conceive by the Holy Spirit and her son would be called Yeshua (Joshua/Jesus), meaning 'God saves' or 'God is salvation.'

Mary's pregnancy created a problem for her espoused husband-to-be Joseph. Being a good man he decided to separate or divorce quietly and not make a fuss now Mary was pregnant. An angel intervened in a dream and explained about the miraculous pregnancy and that Mary's son would be named Yeshua (Joshua/Jesus) because he would save his people from their sins. Matthew wrote that it fulfilled Isaiah's prophecy:

> 'Look, the virgin shall conceive and bear a son,
> and they shall name him Emmanuel'
> which means, 'God is with us.' (Matthew 1:23; Isaiah 9:6)

The great love story burst into history through holy, miraculous conception. Excited at her news, Mary journeyed

---

[10] Acts 5:36-37.

[11] Luke 1:5-24.

about 100km (64 miles) south to visit her relatives Elizabeth and Zechariah near Jerusalem. Old Elizabeth declared that her baby John leaped in her womb when she heard Mary's news.[12] Mary stayed with Elizabeth and her dumb husband for three months till John was born (when Zechariah spoke again). They believed Gabriel's word that John would, in the spirit of Elijah, announce the coming of the Lord. Those two women, supernaturally blessed, carried the wonder of God's loving purposes in their wombs.

This came in the fullness of time.[13] Previous history pointed to Jesus' coming as the Messiah, the Christ, God's Son. We now date history from that birth.

---

[12] Luke 1:26-45.

[13] Galatians 4:4; Ephesians 1:10.

His Birth

Historian Luke gives us details of the birth. The Roman Empire declared a census and all the men (the ones they counted then) had to go to their place of origin. Joseph, descended from King David, had to go to Bethlehem, David's hometown. So pregnant Mary journeyed south once again, this time with Joseph to Bethlehem which is nestled in the hills 12km (8 miles) south of Jerusalem. Today Bethlehem is like a southern suburb of the modern sprawling city of Jerusalem.

Luke's story identifies the time of that census and Jesus' birth. Around 500 years later in AD 525 a monk named Dionysius Exiguus introduced the AD system (*anno domini,* Latin for 'in the year of the Lord') with BC used for the years Before Christ. Modern reckoning places Christ's birth at around 4 or 6 BC. In recent years many publications use the alternative Common Era, CE, and 'Before Common Era, BCE. It's very significant that the Common Era dates from the time of the birth of Jesus.

Relatives in crowded Bethlehem had no room in their guest room so Joseph and Mary used a stable and rested their tiny baby boy in an animals' feeding box, a manger. Modern translations correctly note that there was no room in the guest room so Mary gave birth to her firstborn son in the stable. "She wrapped him in cloths and placed him in a manger because there was no guest room available for them."[14] The tradition of

---

[14] Luke 2:7 (NIV).

no room in the 'inn' dates from the King James Version translation of 1611.

Shepherds in the nearby hills around Bethlehem had quite a night! They saw and heard an angel announce the unique birth, directing them to the baby in the manger. The angel announced a Saviour, the Messiah, and Lord, born in the town of David. To their further astonishment, a host of angels suddenly appeared as well, all giving glory to God.

Those shepherds found the baby in the stable and began telling everyone the amazing things they had seen and heard. It's interesting and significant that the unblemished lambs being prepared for the annual sacrifices in the Temple were born and shepherded among the flocks of Bethlehem. A title for Jesus is the Lamb of God who was sacrificed for us.

People in those times often overlooked shepherds, regarding them as inferior, as was young David before them in those same hills. There Samuel anointed David to be king and there David's greater Son was born king.[15]

Joseph and Mary stayed in Bethlehem, Joseph's ancestral town. Carpenters could find work readily for there were always homes and furniture needing to be built or repaired.

Surprisingly, about a year or just over a year later, Wise Men, astrologers from the East, turned up at their home in Bethlehem. They had been tracking an unusual star and believed it signified the birth of a great king. Naturally, they went to the capital, Jerusalem, looking for the new king, to King Herod's astonishment and alarm. The scholars he consulted said that their great king would be from Bethlehem. Scholars were

---

[15] 1 Samuel 16:11-13.

familiar with the messianic prophecies of Micah, a contemporary of Isaiah (both prophesying about the promised Messiah), speaking and writing before the fall of the northern kingdom of Israel to Assyria in 722 BC, but promising a remnant would return who would see God's eternal kingdom established. They knew Micah 4:1-5 and 5:1-5 (without chapter and verse then as those were added to Greek and other translations from 1551). It included this prophecy:

> 2 But you, O Bethlehem of Ephrathah,
> who are is one of the little clans of Judah,
> from you shall come forth for me
> one who is to rule in Israel,
> whose origin is from of old,
> from ancient days.
> 3 Therefore he shall give them up until the time
> when she who is in labour has brought forth;
> then the rest of his kindred shall return
> to the people of Israel.
> 4 And he shall stand and feed his flock in the strength of
> the LORD,
> in the majesty of the name of the LORD his God.
> And they shall live secure, for now, he shall be great
> to the ends of the earth;
> 5 and he shall be the one of peace.
> (Micah 5:2-5)

Another well-known messianic prophecy from 700 years before its fulfillment about a great Davidic king declared:

> For unto us, a Child is born,
> Unto us a Son is given;
> And the government will be upon His shoulder.

And His name will be called
Wonderful, Counsellor, Mighty God,
Everlasting Father, Prince of Peace.
7 Of the increase of *His* government and peace
There will be no end,
Upon the throne of David and over His kingdom,
To order it and establish it with judgment and justice
From that time forward, even forever.
The zeal of the LORD of hosts will perform this.
(Isaiah 9:6-7 NKJV)

The Wise Men and their entourage saw the star shining over the house in Bethlehem, south of Jerusalem and worshipped the baby king there. They gave Mary and Joseph invaluable gifts of gold, frankincense, and myrrh, which certainly helped them through their sudden refugee status.

A dream warned those international visitors not to report back to Herod, as he had requested, so they took another route back east, bypassing Jerusalem.

An angel appeared again to Joseph in a dream, warning him of Herod's plan to destroy the baby king. The angel told Joseph to escape to Egypt and stay there until he was told to return. They packed quickly and left that night.

Matthew tells how in his fury Herod killed the boys up to two years old in Bethlehem. Herod had a reputation for killing anyone threatening his rule including three of his own sons and one of his wives.

Jewish historian Flavius Josephus described the infamous King Herod the Great as a successful builder in his youth who became increasingly paranoid and ruthless during the final decade of his 36-year reign. He renovated and expanded the Second Temple built by returning exiles around 516 BC, restoring it to the size of the First Temple built by Solomon, and his teams eventually doubled the size of the sandstone Temple Mount with the Antonia fortress at its northern end. His many palace fortresses included one in Jerusalem and another at Masada by the Dead Sea, the place of the last stand of Jews against the Roman invasion of AD 70. Herod the Great, from an Idumaean father, raised as a Jew, governed under Rome's rule.

His Boyhood

The young boy became a refugee, around a year old, escaping Herod's wrath by fleeing with Mary and Joseph to Egypt. So it is likely that Jesus had an early multi-cultural and multi-lingual boyhood among the Jewish diaspora based in Cairo Egypt. They remained there until after Herod's death.

Then in another dream, an angel informed Joseph of the death of those who wanted the child killed and directed him back to the land of Israel. God warned him in a dream so he did not return to Judea where Archelaus, Herod's son ruled, but instead returned again to Nazareth in Galilee.

The family became well-known around Nazareth. The trade of carpenters can also be translated as builder, artisan, stone worker, and metal worker. Jesus (Joshua) and his brothers James (Jacob in Greek), Joseph, Simon, and Judah (or Jude) would learn the family business and care for their sisters. Imagine your older brother being as wise, honest, caring, and loving as Jesus. The townspeople knew him as a carpenter and the son of a carpenter.[16]

As adults, after Jesus' death and resurrection, those brothers and other relatives such as Mary and Mary's sister and her sons joined the company of Jesus' followers. James (Jacob) and Judah (Jude) wrote short, strong, practical, pastoral letters to guide believers, now included in our Bibles.

---

[16] Mark 6:3; Matthew 13:55.

Jesus walked to Jerusalem regularly. Devout Jews journeyed to Jerusalem for each of their three major feasts, Passover and Pentecost around April-May and Tabernacles in October. Jesus attended the Passover feast as a boy of 12, spending extra days in the temple after the annual festival, discussing the Scriptures he had come to fulfil. The scholars were amazed at his understanding and his questions.

Boys of 12, then as now, could recite large passages of their Scriptures, including from the Torah (the five books of Moses) and the Psalms as well as the Prophets. They would be questioned about their understanding and could submit their own questions to the priests and scholars. No wonder Jesus stayed an extra three days in those temple discussions and was surprised that his 'parents' didn't know where he would be. He gave them a loving reminder about his heavenly Father when Mary said "Look, your father and I have been searching for you in great anxiety."[17]

A pure, strong, alert, and gracious boy, Jesus studied his destiny as revealed in the Scriptures and continually embraced his Father's loving purpose for him. Growing up as a teenager, he remained loyal and subject to his human parents while always fulfilling his heavenly Father's will.

He would know the significance of those annual Passover celebrations. They not only recalled God's mighty and loving mercy in saving his people from slavery in Egypt but also pointed to the ultimate sacrifice of God's Son as the Lamb of God who takes away the sin of the world. Exodus 12 tells the story of the first Passover.

---

[17] Luke 2:41-52.

The Lord said to Moses and Aaron in the land of Egypt: 2 This month shall mark for you the beginning of months; it shall be the first month of the year for you. 3 Tell the whole congregation of Israel that on the tenth of this month they are to take a lamb for each family, a lamb for each household. 4 If a household is too small for a whole lamb, it shall join its closest neighbour in obtaining one; the lamb shall be divided in proportion to the number of people who eat of it. 5 Your lamb shall be without blemish, a year-old male; you may take it from the sheep or from the goats. 6 You shall keep it until the fourteenth day of this month; then the whole assembled congregation of Israel shall slaughter it at twilight. 7 They shall take some of the blood and put it on the two doorposts and the lintel of the houses in which they eat it. 8 They shall eat the lamb that same night; they shall eat it roasted over the fire with unleavened bread and bitter herbs. 9 Do not eat any of it raw or boiled in water, but roasted over the fire, with its head, legs, and inner organs. 10 You shall let none of it remain until the morning; anything that remains until the morning you shall burn. 11 This is how you shall eat it: your loins girded, your sandals on your feet, and your staff in your hand; and you shall eat it hurriedly. It is the Passover of the Lord. 12 For I will pass through the land of Egypt that night, and I will strike down every firstborn in the land of Egypt, both human beings and animals; on all the gods of Egypt I will execute judgments: I am the Lord. 13 The blood shall be a sign for you on the houses where you live: when I see the blood, I will pass over you, and no plague shall destroy you when I strike the land of Egypt. (Exodus 12:1-13)

The unblemished lamb, killed in the late afternoon of the 14th of Nisan would be eaten at the Passover or Seder meal on the 15th of Nisan that same evening because the new day began after sunset.

That day was the first day of a week of the Feast of Unleavened Bread which Jesus and his family and friends would celebrate annually in Jerusalem, beginning with the Passover meal, eating the sacrificial Paschal lamb.

Passover, a spring festival, begins at the full moon after the northern vernal equinox. In the Northern Hemisphere the vernal equinox falls around March 20 or 21 as the sun crosses the equator going north, the first day of the month of Nisan.

So the Feast began on the 15th and ended on the 21st of Nisan (usually early April). All leaven, whether in bread or other mixture, was prohibited and they ate only unleavened bread. It symbolized both the Hebrews' suffering while in bondage, and their haste when they left Egypt in the Exodus.

Jesus participated in the annual festivals in Jerusalem, particularly those associated with the three of Passover, Pentecost, and Tabernacles. Through his youth and into manhood, Jesus would journey to Jerusalem at least three times each year to celebrate these feasts, as did all the devout men of Israel.

God gave Moses the dates and details of the annual festivals as summarized in Leviticus 23. Here is a brief overview of those festivals.

1 Passover *(Pesach) - Nisan 14-15* (March/April)

2 Unleavened Bread *(Chag Hamotzi) - Nisan 15-22*

3 First Fruits *(Yom Habikkurim) - Nisan 16-17*

4 Pentecost *(Shavuot) - Sivan 6-7* (May/June)

5 Trumpets *(Yom Teruah)* - *Tishri 1*
(September/October)

6 Atonement *(Yom Kippur)* - *Tishri 10*

7 Tabernacles *(Sukkot)* - *Tishri 15-22*

The Spring Festivals

(1) Passover. The festival year began with the full moon at Passover on the 14th day of the first month (Nisan 14) when the unblemished lamb was slain, celebrating how the angel of death 'passed over' the homes with the blood of the lamb on their door post and lintel. Jesus is our Passover Lamb of God.

(2) Unleavened Bread. This feast began on the next day (Nisan 15) and lasted for seven days. They ate only food without yeast or leaven for that week. Jesus lived without sin, unblemished and pure.

(3) First Fruits. Celebrated on the day after the Sabbath, they brought the early crops of wheat and barley to wave the sheaf before the Lord. They sacrificed Passover lambs on the 14th of Nisan, then the first day of Unleavened Bread was the 15th with the Feast of First Fruits celebrated after the Sabbath. Jesus rose on that day, the first fruit of everlasting life.

(4) Pentecost. On the Sunday after the seventh Sabbath (50 days after the Passover Sabbath) they offered two loaves of bread with leaven/yeast and new meat offerings, marking the beginning of the summer harvest. God's Spirit was poured out on that day after Jesus' death and resurrection.

The Autumn/Fall Festivals

(5) Trumpets. The 1st day of the seventh month (Tishri 1) was celebrated by blowing the ram's horn. The trumpet was the signal for the field workers to come into the Temple. One day, the trumpet will sound, the dead will be raised, and we shall be changed at the Lord's return. (1 Corinthians 15:52)

(6) Atonement. This highest of holy days fell on the 10th day of the seventh month. A day of fasting and sacrifices, it was the only time once a year when the High Priest sprinkled the blood of the sacrifice on the golden mercy seat of the Ark of the Covenant in the Holy of Holies behind the thick curtain in the tabernacle and then later in the temple. The priests released a goat, dedicated to God, into freedom, symbolically carrying the people's sins away, never to return. That's how we got the term scapegoat.[18] Jesus is our atoning sacrifice and takes our sin away.

(7) Tabernacles. The 15th day of the seventh month commenced a week of celebrating in booths, a reminder of God's care for them during the 40 years of Israel's wandering in the wilderness. He led them with a bright cloud above the tabernacle and a pillar of fire at night. He leads us by his Spirit.

A Winter Festival

The Feast of Dedication (Hanukah) in December celebrated the cleansing of the temple in 165 BC when olive oil burned for eight days during the Maccabean revolt against the Greek empire. Jesus attended this optional feast before his final Passover sacrifice the following April.

---

[18] Leviticus 16; 23:26-32; Numbers 29:7-11.

Throughout his youth and into manhood, Jesus would journey with his family and friends from Galilee, along the wide Jordan valley, to Jericho and up the hills into Jerusalem for the three main annual festivals of a week at Passover, a weekend at Pentecost, and over a week at Tabernacles.

They would visit relatives in and around Jerusalem, including Mary's relative Elizabeth, her husband Zechariah, and their anointed son John who was filled with the Spirit from his birth. John knew that Jesus was unique and sinless, but he did not realize that Jesus was indeed the longed-for Messiah until the Spirit of God came upon Jesus when John baptized him.

God's glory filled the human Jesus. His disciple John wrote, "We have seen his glory ... full of grace and truth." At the Last Supper, on the Jewish day he died, Jesus said, "Whoever has seen me has seen the Father." The letter to the Hebrews adds, "He is the reflection of God's glory and the exact imprint of God's very being."[19]

God walked among us in the person of his one and only Son. Some believed in him and followed him. Many did not. It's the same today.

---

[19] John 1:14; 14:9; Hebrews 1:3.

2 MINISTRY BEGINS

Jesus was controversial from the beginning.

He survived many assassination attempts. Two kings, father and son, wanted to kill him. His own townspeople attempted to push him over a cliff. Furious people in Jerusalem tried to stone him more than once. Religious leaders plotted to kill him many times.[20]

But Jesus chose the time, day, and place of his sacrificial death on the cross.

Tension rose. Many believed that the famous, radical young prophet from the rural hills of the village of Nazareth in the north was the long-awaited Messiah, the Christ. That ancient title Messiah (Hebrew) or Christ (Greek) meant God's Anointed One. People hoped their Messiah would free them from the tyranny of the Roman Empire and establish his everlasting kingdom. He did, but not as they expected.

Some people, like the Zealots, wanted to fight to free their nation. Roman soldiers savagely crucified these insurrectionists as a public demonstration of the futility of opposing their Empire. One disciple of the young prophet was Simon the Zealot.

Other people, such as many Jewish leaders, co-operated with their Roman overlords, hoping to keep the peace and prevent further invasion and destruction. One of the radical prophet's

---

[20] Matthew 2:13; Luke 13:31; Luke 4:29; John 8:59, 10:31; Matthew 12:14, 26:4; Mark 11:18; Luke 19:47.

disciples was Matthew who had been a tax collector for Rome. People regarded tax collectors as traitors.

Other disciples of the popular prophet ran a productive fishing business in Galilee, owning boats and employing many fishermen. Some of them returned temporarily to their business after the traumatic and confusing events of their leader's arrest, torture, and public execution.

This radical young prophet annoyed the Jewish leaders. He broke so many of their strict religious laws and traditions. He freely welcomed all kinds of people and was widely known as a friend of prostitutes and sinners including traitors like tax collectors. He visited their homes. He welcomed sinners to join him in the homes of strict religious leaders who were shocked, appalled, and angered.

Jewish historian Josephus noted Jesus' popularity in his account of Jewish history. The *Testimonium Flavianum* (the testimony of Flavius Josephus), the name given to the passage in his *Antiquities of the Jews,* written around AD 93–94, in Book 18, Chapter 3, Section 3, says this (probably edited):

> About this time there lived Jesus, a wise man, if indeed one ought to call him a man. For he was one who performed surprising deeds and was a teacher of such people as accept the truth gladly. He won over many Jews and many of the Greeks. He was the Christ. And when, upon the accusation of the principal men among us, Pilate had condemned him to a cross, those who had first come to love him did not cease. He appeared to them spending a third day restored to life, for the prophets of God had foretold these things and a thousand other marvels about him. And the tribe of the Christians, so called after him, has still to this day not disappeared.

There's a lot of debate about the dates of Jesus' ministry and death but one sequence often used is that the first Passover in his ministry was possibly around AD 28 or 29, with the crucifixion around early April of AD 30 or AD 31 (on the Thursday). Scholars debate many other possibilities.

Jesus' public ministry began when he was around 30 after his baptism in the Jordan River and after 40 days of fasting in the Judean desert where he rejected strong temptation. The Jordan flows from the freshwater Lake of Galilee, 210m (700 feet) below sea level, for 100km (60 miles) through the 10km (6 miles) wide Jordan valley to the Dead Sea, 430m (1400 feet) below sea level. This lowest place on earth is about 50km (35 miles) southeast of the mountain city of Jerusalem at about 750m (2,500 feet).

The following map from *Bible History Online* gives a useful picture of Jesus' travels and ministry. Jesus and thousands of others often walked over 100km or around 70 miles between Galilee and Jerusalem, especially for the three main annual Feasts.

Website and publication use is permitted with a link going to **Bible History Online**: https://bible-history.com/maps/palestine-nt-times.

Israel in the New Testament

Bible History Online

I arrange my summary of Jesus' life and ministry in these sections:

1 Birth and Boyhood

2 Ministry Begins

3 First to Second Passovers

4 Second to Third Passovers

5 Passover to Pentecost

This chapter gives you an overview of those years involving the three Passovers and then describes events around the first of those three.

There are many possible sequences and chronologies. One sequence is that Jesus' ministry included three Passovers.

First to Second Passovers

The first Passover occurred after his family, and some of his disciples attended a wedding in Cana where he performed his first miracle of turning water into wine. His family and some early disciples then went to Capernaum on Lake Galilee and joined the crowds going down the wide Jordan valley to Jericho and up the hills to Jerusalem for the Passover. John the Baptist and Jesus were both preaching to the crowds and calling people to turn to God. Jesus explained about faith and new birth to Nicodemus and returned to the Jordan to preach. His disciples also baptized people as a sign of repentance. When Jesus knew that his growing popularity concerned and threatened the Pharisees, he chose to withdraw and returned to Galilee through the hills of Samaria where he talked with the Samaritan woman and to the villagers there.

Jesus began his early ministry in Galilee around his base at Capernaum on the northwest of the Lake of Galilee. He enlisted his first disciples who then joined him, as did many others, including women who supported them.

The main ministry in Galilee included sending his twelve close disciples on mission and it covers most of the ministry of Jesus in Galilee.

Second to Third Passovers

The second Passover followed the beheading of John the Baptist in prison, and when Jesus withdrew with his disciples across the lake. Crowds, who were gathering for the Passover pilgrimage, followed them around the northern shore, and he healed the sick, preached, and fed them from a boy's lunch. They wanted to make him their king immediately, but he withdrew to the hills to pray, and later walked on the stormy water, and joined the disciples in their boat which immediately reached the shore. This time at the Passover in Jerusalem tension rose sharply as Jesus clashed with religious leaders.

The final ministry in Galilee culminates in the Transfiguration in the mountains near Caesarea Philippi, where he talked with Moses and Elijah about his approaching departure from the earth. Jesus prepared for his last journey to Jerusalem. He sent seventy of his followers on a mission to the places he was about to visit on his final journey to Jerusalem.

His last journey through Galilee and Judea included visits to Jerusalem for the Feast of Tabernacles around September/October, and for the Feast of Dedication in the winter of December, now called Hanukkah.[21] His final journey to Jerusalem for the Passover in April followed raising Lazarus from death in Bethany and encounters with Bartimaeus and Zacchaeus in Jericho.

That later ministry in Judea included Jesus' final journey to Jerusalem through the region of southern Jordan and Jericho, up to the hills of Bethany, and on to nearby Jerusalem.

Passover to Pentecost

The third and final Passover involved Jesus' death and resurrection. He then appeared to many of his followers during forty days until his ascension.

The final ministry in Jerusalem, known as Passion Week or Holy Week began with Jesus' triumphant entry on what is now called Palm Sunday. The gospels devote about one-third of their text to that final week. Then, for just over a month, the risen Lord often appeared to his followers.

Jesus' ministry probably covers those three Passovers, as John's Gospel suggests: the first described in John 2, the second in John 6:4, and the third (the Last Supper and crucifixion) in John 11:55; 12:1; 13:1; 18:28, 39; and 19:14. All the Gospels describe that final week in great detail.

Peter, the leader among the disciples, preached at the Pentecost Feast, fifty days after the Passover Feast and around three thousand people believed. Peter broke strict Jewish laws when he later preached in the spacious home of the Roman centurion

---

[21] John 7:1–52; 10:22–42.

Cornelius in Caesarea. He told how the good news of God's grace is for everyone, not only for Jews.

Peter summarized Jesus' ministry this way:

> Then Peter began to speak to them: 'I truly understand that God shows no partiality, 35 but in every nation, anyone who fears him and does what is right is acceptable to him. 36 You know the message he sent to the people of Israel, preaching peace by Jesus Christ—he is Lord of all. 37 That message spread throughout Judea, beginning in Galilee after the baptism that John announced: 38 how God anointed Jesus of Nazareth with the Holy Spirit and with power; how he went about doing good and healing all who were oppressed by the devil, for God was with him. 39 We are witnesses to all that he did both in Judea and in Jerusalem. They put him to death by hanging him on a tree; 40 but God raised him on the third day and allowed him to appear, 41 not to all the people but to us who were chosen by God as witnesses, and who ate and drank with him after he rose from the dead. 42 He commanded us to preach to the people and to testify that he is the one ordained by God as judge of the living and the dead. 43 All the prophets testify about him that everyone who believes in him receives forgiveness of sins through his name.
> (Acts 10:34-42)

This book provides you with a condensed overview of some key biographical events in Jesus' life and ministry. It gives you one of many possible sequences but correlates with various harmonies of the Gospels.

The Gospel writers give us Gospels, not a biography. They proclaim the good news of the Saviour of the world. So they do not always clarify the sequence of events. You can read the details of all the events in the Gospels themselves. I find it inspiring to read a chapter of a Gospel each day, beginning with chapter one on the first day of the month, for convenience, and roaming as led. I like to note a key thought from the reading in my diary each day.

What follows here is a harmonized story of God's love shown to us in Jesus the Messiah, God's Son, who reveals God's love and glory.

Early Ministry in Judea

John the Baptist, the rugged wilderness prophet wearing camel's hair tied with a leather strap, eating a diet of a range of locusts sweetened with wild honey, came in the spirit and power of Elijah to prepare the way for the coming of the Lord.[22] He called people to get ready, to turn from sin and be baptized in the Jordan River.

Jesus came to be baptized, obeying his Father's requirement. John was surprised and felt that Jesus should baptize him, but Jesus insisted on obeying his Father. As he came up from the water the Spirit of God came upon him like a dove. John saw it and realized that Jesus was indeed God's Anointed One, the Messiah, God's Son, the Lamb of God who takes away the sin of the world. God's Spirit came upon and filled Jesus, God said, "This is my Son, the Beloved, with whom I am well pleased."[23]

Jesus the Anointed One, conceived miraculously by God's Spirit, was now anointed, empowered, and baptized by and in God's Holy Spirit for ministry. During his 40 days of prayer and fasting at the beginning of that ministry, he was tempted to misuse that anointing and power to feed himself, to rule the world, and to make a display. He resisted temptation, quoting relevant

---

[22] Leviticus 11:22; 2 Kings 1:8; Malachi 4:5-6; Matthew 3; 11:7-11; Mark 1:1-8; Luke 1:15-17; 3:2-20; John 1:23.

[23] Matthew 3:17; Luke 3:22.

Scriptures. Then his ministry began, empowered and led by the Holy Spirit.[24]

Jesus was fully man (not super-boy or super-man). He was indeed God's Son but he emptied himself of his rights and became fully human. Now, anointed and empowered by God's Spirit he began his ministry in the power of the Spirit of God. Later on, he empowered his followers with his authority in the same way.[25]

Jesus' early ministry in Judea began with his baptism, his fasting and temptations, and inviting followers to be with him in both Judea in the south and Galilee in the north.

Many people are familiar with Jesus calling disciples around Galilee, but may forget that many of them began following him in the southern Jordan among the crowds responding to John the Baptist, and then also to Jesus.

The multitudes moved freely along the wide fertile Jordan valley with its freshwater river flowing from Lake Galilee. This was the main trading and traveling route, especially during the annual feast times in Jerusalem.

In the beginning, both John the Baptist and Jesus preached in the Jordan Valley and Jesus' disciples also baptized many people who responded. Crowds following Jesus grew rapidly, especially as John referred to Jesus as being God's Son, the Messiah.[26]

Andrew and his brother Simon, whom Jesus called Peter, believed John's word about Jesus and met him. Jesus invited

------

[24] Luke 4:1, 14, 18-19; Matthew 4:1-11.

[25] John 1:32-34; 14:12; Luke 24:49; Acts 2:1-4; Philippians 2:5-11.

[26] John 1:29-34; 3:22-30; 4:1-3.

Philip and Nathanael to join him and soon the word spread. Two others among many who followed Jesus from the time of John's baptizing were Joseph and Matthias.[27]

John rejoiced that Jesus' fame and popularity increased. He insisted that Jesus must increase when he, John, must decrease. So when Jesus journeyed before and after that first Passover following his baptism, increasingly large crowds followed him.

Before that first Passover, a group of them returned to Galilee, and then Jesus joined his family with some of his disciples at the wedding in Cana where they ran out of wine, possibly due to the growing number of Jesus' followers. Jesus turned water into the best wine after his mother urged him to do something to help. This was his first miraculous sign after his empowerment at his baptism. He provided the best wine. Today people often refer to that at weddings. Then Jesus and his family and new followers went on to Capernaum on Lake Galilee.

Following that journey north, Jesus and an increasing number of followers returned along the Jordan Valley, heading towards Jerusalem for the Passover feast. Jesus taught the growing crowds, and his disciples baptized many followers who believed in Jesus the Messiah.

That visit to Jerusalem probably included the famous discussion with the religious leader Nicodemus, a Pharisee, who talked with Jesus at night, probably avoiding the huge daytime crowds. Nicodemus later clashed with many of the Sanhedrin, the ruling council, by supporting Jesus at the Feast of Tabernacles the

---

[27] John 1:35-51; Acts 1:21-23.

following year, and the next year he helped another believer, Joseph of Arimathea, to place Jesus' body in the tomb.[28]

People followed Jesus in many ways. The largest numbers came for healing and help. The young traveling Rabbi's teaching and stories attracted huge crowds. He taught with unusual authority and continually explained how to live life in God's kingdom. He always used parables.[29] His stories were easy to tell to others. Their meaning and significance, however, often puzzled people, including his closest disciples. So Jesus regularly explained their true significance to those who really wanted to understand and live kingdom life.

Even though Jesus was very popular and attracted a huge following he also challenged and confronted people, especially small-minded people stuck in their traditions and unwilling to grasp God's vast love for all people, especially for those caught in sin and for outcasts and outsiders.

Throughout his ministry, Jesus often rebuked his disciples for their narrow-mindedness and arguments about who was greatest or best among his followers. Jesus insisted that the greatest were those who served, who laid down their lives for others, and who truly desired God's glory, not their own glory. Self-denial, not self-indulgence, was his way.

Jesus reprimanded his closest followers when they wanted exalted positions, and when they wanted to punish opponents,

---

[28] John 3:1-21; 7:50-51; 19:39-42.

[29] Matthew 13:34; Mark 4:22, 33-34. Parables included metaphors, similes, allegories, comparisons, riddles, figures of speech and enigmatic sayings to reveal spiritual and eternal truth.

and when they kept children away, and especially when they doubted him or lacked faith.

They, like us, were slow learners. Even on his last night with them at the Last Supper, they still argued about who was greatest, best, or most effective. Jesus confronted them even then by washing their dusty feet, something any of them could have done but apparently none did.[30]

Throughout his life and ministry, Jesus often commended those with faith in him, those who served, and those who honoured and lived for God.

You can study discussions of the biographical sequence of Jesus' life and ministry. Internet Archive gives free downloads of Giuseppe Ricciotti's classic, scholarly book *The Life of Christ* (1947). He gives a detailed chronological sequence of Jesus' life and ministry (translated from Italian): https://archive.org/details/thelifeofchrist_201911.

Scholarly opinions differ widely concerning the sequence of these events, but in this book, I follow early traditional views as one likely option.

---

[30] Luke 22:24-27; John 13:1-17.

3 FIRST TO SECOND PASSOVERS

The Temple on the eastern ridge of Jerusalem stood at the heart of Jewish life. Solomon's Temple (built around 950 BC) was destroyed in 586 BC by Nebuchadnezzar. Jews who were released from captivity under Cyrus of Persia, 70 years later, built the smaller Second Temple from 516 BC. Herod the Great expanded it.

Herod's Temple, begun in 20 BC, enlarged the Temple to its original size and doubled the size of the Temple Mount to around 35 acres with the Roman garrison Antonia Fortress on its northern edge. It took 46 years to complete which may place Jesus' first Passover after his baptism sometime after AD 26. That corresponds with him being around 30 at the beginning of his public ministry, with the date of his birth identified as about 6 or 4 BC.[31]

After that first Passover following his baptism, Jesus and his growing band of disciples returned to the south Jordan where both he and John the Baptist were preaching, proclaiming God's kingdom, and urging people to turn to God. Jesus' fame grew. Concerned religious leaders in Jerusalem doubted that the young prophet and miracle worker from Nazareth could be the longed-for Messiah. When Jesus heard of their concerns and

---

[31] Luke 3:1-2, 23; John 2:20.

opposition he quietly withdrew north again through the inland mountain route to Samaria.

There he met the woman of Samaria at Jacob's well between the surrounding hills and then stayed there for two days explaining God's kingdom to the Samaritans. This surprised even his disciples for Jews had no dealings with Samaritans. Jesus often shocked people with his love and compassion for all people, especially the neglected and outcasts.

Back in Cana Jesus healed a royal official's son in Capernaum with a word. The official believed him and found his son well on his return home.

John 5 tells of Jesus' brief, controversial visit to Jerusalem for one of the feasts, possibly Pentecost, 50 days after Passover. Jesus healed a cripple on a Sabbath at the Pool of Bethesda. The religious leaders angrily interrogated the man because he carried his rolled-up mat on a Sabbath. They couldn't understand God's love and compassion that transcended their man-made rules and legalistic interpretation of Scripture.

Early Ministry in Galilee

The Early Galilean ministry began when Jesus returned to Galilee after John the Baptist was imprisoned.

> Now when Jesus heard that John had been arrested, he withdrew to Galilee. He left Nazareth and made his home in Capernaum by the lake (Matthew 4:12-13).

> Now after John was arrested, Jesus came to Galilee, proclaiming the good news of God, and saying, 'The time is fulfilled, and the kingdom of God has come near; repent, and believe in the good news' (Mark 1:14-15).

> Then Jesus, filled with the power of the Spirit, returned to Galilee, and a report about him spread through all the surrounding country. He began to teach in their synagogues and was praised by everyone (Luke 4:14).

Jesus called his first disciples who began to travel with him. He returned for a visit to Nazareth where his explanation of his own mission and of God's love for all people of all nations offended the townspeople. They were so furious they tried to kill him.[32]

Jesus established his ministry base at Capernaum on the lake where the brothers Andrew and Peter and the brothers James and John had their busy fishing business. Jesus taught in their synagogue, cast out an unclean spirit, and healed Peter's mother-in-law. People were astonished at his teaching because

---

[32] Matthew 4:18-25; Luke 4:15-30.

he spoke with such authority and reports about him spread widely.[33]

Jesus called Matthew (also named Levi) from his tax collecting booth in that area and Matthew also left his profitable business to travel with Jesus. Both Matthew and John eventually wrote about Jesus' teachings and miracles during those journeys together.

Matthew records Jesus' Sermon on the Mount, the first of five discourses in Matthew (See *Kingdom Life in Matthew,* with a free PDF on links in renewaljournal.com). Luke records similar teaching in the Sermon on the Plain. Here I summarise highlights from the Sermon on the Mount and Jesus' radical teaching. God's way of love, as demonstrated in Jesus, confronts and transforms life and society.

The beatitudes turn things upside down. Those who pursue and live in God's kingdom reign are truly blessed.

Jesus judged people by their hearts and intentions. Those who reject or resist God's love for them and for all people are in danger of being condemned to eternal darkness, away from God's light. We are to love our enemies and pray for those who persecute us. We must forgive others just as God forgives us.

Jesus completes the law and the prophets in himself, and living by the golden rule of doing to others what you want them to do for you, fulfills all the law and prophets.[34]

The Lord's Prayer is a model of how to pray, not a means of vain repetition. Current versions of it include words such as these:

---

[33] Mark 1:21-28; Luke 4:31-37.

[34] Matthew 5-7; Luke 6:17-49.

Our Father in heaven, hallowed be Your name.
Your kingdom come, Your will be done on earth as it is in
heaven.
Give us this day our daily bread,
And forgive us our sins as we forgive those who sin
against us.
Lead us away from temptation and deliver us from evil,
For Yours is the kingdom, the power, and the glory,
forever and ever. Amen.

An Aramaic form of that prayer begins, *A'bawoon d'bashmaya,* which means, "Beloved who is everywhere."

Jesus challenged us to live according to God's kingdom and his righteousness above all else and then God would meet our needs. If we live by his teaching it's like building our house on rock, not on sand.

People were amazed and awestruck by Jesus' teaching because he taught them as someone with ultimate authority and not like others who quoted other people. Jesus taught and demonstrated God's way of love for everyone.

Conflicts with religious leaders increased because Jesus associated freely with sinners and healed people on the Sabbath. The strict rules and traditions of religious leaders prohibited associating with people regarded as unclean and prohibited doing any kind of work on a Sabbath.

Jesus reminded them that even on Sabbaths the priests would offer sacrifices, boys were circumcised on the eighth day, and people would rescue animals or water them as needed and help children who fell. Jesus revealed God's love, justice, and compassion in all that he did, including healing people on Sabbath days.

Main Ministry in Galilee

The main Galilean ministry continues from the Sermon on the Mount to the death of John the Baptist (Matthew 8-14). Matthew alternates his narratives about Jesus with passages of Jesus' teaching as in this adapted lectionary summary.

Christ's design for life in God's kingdom

The call of the first disciples (Mt 4:12-23)

The Sermon on the Mount (Mt 5-7)

The spread of God's kingdom

The call of Levi/Matthew (Mt 9:9-13)

The mission sermon (Mt 9:35-10:42)

The mystery of God's kingdom

The revelation to the simple (Mt 11:25-30)

The parable sermon (Mt 13)

God's Kingdom on Earth and the Church

Feeding 5000, Canaanite woman, Peter's confession (Mt 14-17)

The community sermon (Mt 18:15-35)

Authority and invitation: at the final Passover

The final parables, tribute, and greatest commandment (Mt 20-24)

The final sermon (Mt 25)

Jesus' parables upset people. He continually turned things around. For example, the Good Samaritan story praised the hated Samaritan (Jews had no dealings with them) and condemned the respected religious leaders.[35]

Some of Jesus' most famous stories grew from opposition to his teaching and to his compassion for everyone, especially for sinners. Three well-known examples are the stories of the lost sheep, the lost coin, and the lost son (the prodigal son).[36] Why did Jesus tell those stories? Luke tells us why. Jesus welcomed the despised tax collectors regarded as traitors, and the notorious sinners including prostitutes, often eating with them. Religious leaders and scholars strongly criticized Jesus for that so he responded with those stories.

Jesus told many parables or allegories drawn from everyday life. For example, he talked about seeds sown on hard, stony, thorny, and good ground. He explained that God's Word at times fell on hard-hearted people, shallow–minded people, worldly-wise people, or open-hearted people, with varying results. It produced good fruit in good lives.

After praying all night, Jesus chose twelve disciples from among his many followers and commissioned them to preach, heal the sick, and cast out unclean spirits, just as he did.[37] A song that many of us sang as children, based on Matthew 10:2-4, to the tune of 'Bringing in the Sheaves,' lists the names of the disciples:

> There were 12 disciples Jesus called to help him,
> Simon Peter, Andrew, James, his brother John,
> Philip, Thomas, Matthew, James the son of Alpheus,

---

[35] Luke 10:25-36.

[36] Luke 15.

[37] Matthew 10:1-15; Luke 9:1-6.

Thaddaeus, Simon, Judas, and Bartholomew.
He has called us too, He has called us too.
We are his disciples. I am one; are you?
He has called us too, He has called us too.
We are his disciples, we his work must do.

Jesus sent his disciples and others out to preach and heal, showing God's love and compassion for everyone. Many women travelled with Jesus and his team and supported them with food and clothing. Some of them were from rich families.[38]

John the Baptist in prison sent two of his disciples to ask Jesus if he were truly the Messiah so Jesus summarized what he did in healing and teaching as evidence of his messiahship.[39]

Jesus constantly showed his great love for all people by forgiving and healing people, and large crowds flocked to him.

> When he saw the crowds, he had compassion for them, because they were harassed and helpless, like sheep without a shepherd. (Matthew 9:36)

> Many crowds followed him, and he cured all of them. (Matthew 12:15)

> And wherever he went, into villages or cities or farms, they laid the sick in the marketplaces, and begged him that they might touch even the fringe of his cloak; and all who touched it were healed. (Mark 6:56)

> And all in the crowd were trying to touch him, for power came out from him and healed all of them. (Luke 6:19)

---

[38] Luke 8:1.

[39] Matthew 11:2-6.

The Gospels give us many accounts of Jesus healing people, setting people free, and even raising the dead.

He taught and traveled from his base in Capernaum, visiting many towns and villages. He healed a centurion's servant with just a word at the soldier's request. Jesus praised him for his faith and his understanding of authority. At Nain, he raised a widow's son from death.

He stilled a storm on the lake after his alarmed disciples woke him from his sleep. Across the lake, he set two demonized madmen free. Back again at Capernaum, he healed more people including forgiving and healing a paralyzed man on his mat, let down through the roof by four friends because they could not get in through the crowd. Having a former carpenter there would be handy for roof repairs! Religious leaders criticized him for forgiving sin, calling it blasphemy.

Jesus healed a woman who had been haemorrhaging for twelve years and raised the synagogue's leader Jairus' 12-year-old daughter from death. As he left their house two blind men followed him into the next house and he healed them because they believed. After they left people brought him a man afflicted with a dumb spirit whom he healed but religious leaders accused him of using occult power.[40]

Later, Jesus set free a blind and dumb man, but again Pharisees accused him of using occult power. Jesus strongly warned them not to accuse the Holy Spirit like that or they could not be

---

[40] Matthew 9:18-34; Mark 5:21-43; Luke 8:40-56.

forgiven. Jesus reminded them that his casting out evil or unclean spirits showed that God's kingdom came in him.[41]

People crowded around Jesus. Many just wanted to touch him to be healed, and they were.[42] At times Jesus and his disciples had no time to eat because of the vast crowds seeking healing.[43] Sometimes Jesus slipped away for time out, time alone. Jesus often rose before dawn to pray alone and sometimes spent all night praying in intimate fellowship with his Father.[44]

John wrote his Gospel around seven powerful signs that demonstrated Jesus' true nature and glory. John focused on Jesus' teaching, built around these signs of his power and authority.

Around the first Passover:

> 1. Turning water into wine (2:1-12)
>
> 2. Healing the nobleman's son (4:46-54)
>
> 3. Healing the man at Bethesda (5:1-47)

Around the second Passover:

> 4. Feeding the 5000 (6:1-4)
>
> 5. Walking on Water (6:15-21)
>
> 6. Healing the Blind Man (9:1-41)
> Around the third Passover:

---

[41] Matthew 12:22-45; Luke 11: 14-26.

[42] Mark 5:56; Matthew 14:36.

[43] Mark 3:20; 6:31.

[44] Mark 1:35; Luke 4:42; 6:12.

7. Raising of Lazarus (11:1-57)

Christ's Resurrection (2:18-22; 20;21)

John's Gospel calls these events signs and shows how Jesus explained that his signs pointed to his divinity and authority as the Son of God.

John also gives us the 'I am' statements of Jesus. His Greek manuscript used a strong emphasis: *"ego eimi"—I alone am,* or *I myself am.* These sayings of Jesus are unique and challenging claims. Those pictures or metaphors upset many people.

1. I am the bread of life ... and anyone who comes to me I will never drive away (John 6:35, just before the second Passover, April).

2. I am the light of the world. Whoever follows me will never walk in darkness but will have the light of life (John 8:12, at the Feast of Tabernacles, October).

3. I am the door/gate for the sheep ... I am the door/gate. Whoever enters by me will be saved, and will come in and go out and find pasture (John 10:7, 9, at the Feast of Dedication, December).

4. I am the good shepherd. The good shepherd lays down his life for the sheep (John 10:11, at the Feast of Dedication, December).

5. I am the resurrection and the life. Those who believe in me, even though they die, will live, and everyone who lives and believes in me will never die. Do you believe this? (John 11:25-26, at Bethany before the final Passover).

6. I am the way, and the truth, and the life. No one comes to the Father except through me (John 14:6, at the Last Supper).

7. I am the true vine, and my Father is the vine-grower. ... I am the vine, you are the branches. Those who abide in me and I in them bear much fruit, because apart from me you can do nothing (John 15:1, 5, at the Last Supper).

When Jesus clashed with scholars in Jerusalem at the Feast of Tabernacles he declared "Before Abraham was, I am" (John 8:58). That infuriated them so much that they picked up stones to throw at him but he slipped away from them.

The claims Jesus made about himself, especially in the last year of his life, increased the Jewish leaders' opposition to him and hatred of him. They regarded those claims as blasphemy. Increasingly they plotted to kill him.

Their view of their anticipated Messiah differed widely from this radical, miracle-working prophet who broke so many of their traditions and claimed that God was his Father. Jesus confronted, them, pointing out that their own Scriptures described him:

> You study the Scriptures diligently because you think that in them you have eternal life. These are the very Scriptures that testify about me, yet you refuse to come to me to have life. (John 5:39-40 NIV)

4 SECOND TO THIRD PASSOVERS

Final Ministry in Galilee

The Final Galilean ministry began after John the Baptist was beheaded.

Following Herod the Great's death, Emperor Augustus divided Herod's kingdom among three of his sons. **Archelaus** ruled Samaria, Judea, and Idumea for about nine years until Emperor Augustus replaced him with governors from Rome, including the procurator Pontius Pilate who ruled the enlarged province of Judea during AD 26–36. Herod **Antipas** became the tetrarch of Galilee and Peraea and ruled during the ministry of Jesus. **Philip**, the tetrarch of territories north and east of the Jordan River, was divorced by his wife Herodias who then married Antipas.

John the Baptist publicly rebuked Antipas who acted quickly and savagely against any sign of opposition or rebellion. He imprisoned and later beheaded John although he respected and feared him. His daughter's dance at a state banquet for his birthday pleased Antipas so much that he publicly offered her what she desired, and at her mother's instruction, she asked for John's head. Antipas regretfully complied because of his public vow.

When Jesus heard of John's death he sailed privately to a solitary place near Bethsaida on the north of the lake. It followed a time when he had sent 70 of his followers on a mission in pairs to places he was going to visit and they reported back about people being healed and set free.

Large crowds had gathered because it was near Passover and multitudes were assembling for the journey from Galilee along the Jordan valley to Jerusalem. The crowds followed the boat with Jesus and his disciples around the northern shore of Galilee. Jesus had compassion for them, healed the sick, taught them, and fed the crowd of over 5,000 from a boy's lunch, the first of two times he fed crowds miraculously. They wanted to make him their king there and then.

He sent the disciples off in their boat and went to the hills to pray alone. That night he returned to them, walking on the water, as did Peter when he looked at Jesus. Jesus held him when he sank. As they walked into the boat together, the wind ceased and they were all immediately at the shore. The amazed disciples worshipped him declaring, "Truly you are the Son of God."[45]

Later, Jesus journeyed north to Tyre and Sidon on the Mediterranean where he healed the Canaanite's daughter even though that was beyond his mission to Israel. Jesus then returned to Lake Galilee. After three days of healing and teaching, he miraculously fed over 4,000 from one meal. He moved on to the Decapolis, ten towns southeast of Galilee, healing and teaching.

The crowds, and even Jesus' disciples, expected him to be their triumphant king, a conqueror who would free them from Roman

---

[45] Matthew 14:22-33; Mark 6:45-52; John 6:15-21.

rule and establish his kingdom in Israel (John 6:15; Acts 1:6). But his everlasting kingdom differed from their ideas.

The tyranny of Rome's empire, and the heavy taxes imposed on subject people, stirred resentment and anger among many Jews. They longed for their promised Messiah to set them free, and the crowds saw in Jesus a great hope for a new, powerful, free, and just kingdom.

Jesus emphasized that God's eternal kingdom was in our hearts by faith in himself as God's Son and our Saviour.

Jesus prophesied his death three times

Jesus told his disciples three times about his approaching death and resurrection, but they didn't understand. Confused and distressed they were afraid to ask him about it:

First, at Caesarea Philippi (Matthew 16:21-28; Mark 8:31-38; Luke 9:21-27).

Second, in Galilee (Matthew 17:22-23; Mark 9:30-32; Luke 9:43-45).

Third, near Jerusalem (Matthew 20:17-19; Mark 10:32-34; Luke 18:31-34).

(1) Jesus' Galilean ministry culminated in taking the disciples away from the crowds into the hills north of Lake Galilee. At Caesarea Philippi, toward Mt Hermon, Jesus told them about his impending death. After praying, Jesus asked his disciples who people thought he was. Popular opinions ranged from him being John the Baptist raised from the dead to Elijah or another prophet raised to life. When Jesus asked them what they thought, Peter, their natural leader, declared that Jesus was

indeed the Messiah, the Christ, the messianic king anointed by God to come and establish his eternal kingdom.

Jesus reminded Peter that God had revealed that to him. Then Jesus told them he would be going to Jerusalem again and would be arrested, tortured, and killed. Peter strenuously objected to that idea and earned a sharp rebuke from his loving Lord.

Six days later Jesus climbed further into the mountains with Peter, James, and John and was transfigured, shining in heavenly glory. He talked with Moses and Elijah about his approaching departure from the earth.

Both Moses and Elijah had left the earth in unusual ways. Moses saw the Promised Land from the mountains of Nebo, southeast of the Jordan Valley after he had led the Israelites for forty years. God talked with him as a man talked with his close friend. Moses handed his leadership to Joshua, who led the Israelites into their Promised Land. Moses went off alone with God who buried his body. Moses, on that mountain at the transfiguration, was in the Promised Land, seeing the fulfillment of his calling, and his prophecy about a great prophet to come, now fulfilled in Jesus, God's Son.[46]

Elijah had been taken up to heaven by a whirlwind when horses and a chariot of fire separated him from his disciple Elisha who then continued in that anointed and powerful ministry of signs and wonders. John the Baptist had come in the spirit of Elijah, and now Elijah was there talking with Jesus about how Jesus would fulfill his messianic mission through his atoning death. Many scholars interpret that encounter as Moses and Elijah

---

[46] Deuteronomy 18:15.

representing the law and prophets which were all fulfilled in Jesus.

Peter, James, and John witnessed the Transfiguration where Moses and Elijah talked with Jesus about his coming departure and God spoke from the cloud of glory: This is my Son, my Beloved, whom I love; listen to him. (Matthew 17:1-8; see Mark 9:2-8; Luke 9:28-36; 2 Peter 1:16-18).

The Transfiguration, a pivotal event told around the middle of the Gospels, marks the beginning of Jesus' final journey to Jerusalem and to his death. (Matthew 16:21; cf. Mark 8:31-32; Luke 9:21-22)

(2) After the Transfiguration as they journeyed south, Jesus again predicted his death. "They went on from there and passed through Galilee. And he did not want anyone to know, for he was teaching his disciples, saying to them, 'The Son of Man is going to be delivered into the hands of men, and they will kill him. And when he is killed, after three days he will rise.' But they did not understand the saying, and were afraid to ask him." (Mark 9:30-32)

Matthew says that the disciples were greatly distressed. Luke adds that his disciples did not understand, and the meaning was hidden from them. (Matthew 17:22-23; Luke 9:43-45)

(3) Finally, as they approached Jerusalem, Jesus told his disciples what would happen to him there.

> While Jesus was going up to Jerusalem, he took the twelve disciples aside by themselves, and said to them on the way, 'See, we are going up to Jerusalem, and the Son of Man will be handed over to the chief priests and scribes, and they will condemn him to death; then they will hand him over to the Gentiles to be mocked and

flogged and crucified; and on the third day he will be raised.' (Matthew 20:17-19; cf. Mark 10:32-34; Luke 18:31-34)

Jesus referred to himself as the Son of Man, not only to show his humanity but it was also a messianic title from the book of Daniel. There, one like a son of man is given dominion and glory and a kingdom that shall not be destroyed.[47]

---

[47] Daniel 7:13-14.

Later Ministry in Judea

During his lengthy final journey south Jesus commissioned 70 of his followers to go in pairs ahead of him to tell about God's kingdom, heal the sick, and cast out unclean spirits.[48] They experienced God's power in their ministry like Jesus did in his.

As the crowds and also the opposition increased Jesus attended two further feasts in Jerusalem, the Feast of Tabernacles in September/October, and the Feast of Dedication in December.

(1) The seven-day **Feast of Tabernacles** or **Feast of Booths** (Sukkot) around September/October celebrated the end of the summer harvests and also God's care for his people when they lived in booths during the Exodus from Egypt. When Jesus' brothers were leaving for that feast they encouraged Jesus to go public in Judea, because he spent most of his time in Galilee away from the hub of religious life and authority in Jerusalem. At that time his brothers did not fully believe he was actually the promised Messiah. Later on, after his resurrection they did believe and became leaders in the church. Two of them wrote the brief letters of James and Jude.[49]

Jesus went late and secretly to that Feast of Tabernacles. Some leaders wanted him arrested and executed. During the feast, they sent temple guards to arrest him but the guards were astounded by him and did nothing.

Each afternoon of that festival week the priests poured out a libation of water and wine at the temple altar, and during

---

[48] Luke 10:1-24.

[49] Mark 3:20–21; John 7:1–10; James; Jude,

the last and greatest day of the feast (possibly when the water was being poured out) Jesus boldly proclaimed, "If anyone is thirsty, let them come to me and drink. Whoever believes in me, as the Scripture has said, streams of living water will flow from within them,"[50] He was describing what the Holy Spirit would do in believers' lives.

Arguments about Jesus ran hot. Some people thought he was the prophet that Moses predicted. Others believed he was the promised Messiah. The temple guards, sent to arrest Jesus returned without him, saying that no one spoke like he did. The Pharisees accused the guards of being fooled by Jesus. Nicodemus, however, defended Jesus' right to be heard. They argued with him declaring that in the Scriptures no prophet would come from Galilee.[51] Apparently, they had not done their homework or carefully researched the birthplace of Jesus.

John's Gospel tells how the next day as Jesus taught in the temple the Pharisees and teachers of the law brought in a woman caught in adultery. They wanted to trap Jesus reminding him that their law said she should be stoned. Jesus reminded them of their own sin, saying that those without sin could throw the first stone, a statement often adapted now such as those who live in glass houses shouldn't throw stones. Then Jesus wrote in the dust. I wonder what he wrote! My guess is that he wrote Scriptures identifying their sins. They dropped their stones and left, beginning with the eldest who probably had failed the

---

[50] John 7:35.

[51] John 7:37-52; Deuteronomy 18:15-19.

longest. Jesus showed God's immense love, telling the woman that he did not condemn her. He also told her to stop sinning, which was what he consistently told everyone.

Jesus saw a beggar blind from birth, so he spat on the ground, made mud, and smeared it on the man's eyes. He sent him down to the Pool of Siloam to wash. It was on a Sabbath and Pharisees were furious about the healing. They heatedly interrogated the man and his parents. That man believed in Jesus so was excommunicated by the religious leaders.

(2) The Winter **Feast of Dedication** in December (now called Hanukah) celebrated the Maccabean victory over the Seleucid-Greeks in 165 BC when olive oil burned in the cleansed temple miraculously for eight days till more could be made. The feast celebrations still include lighting eight lamps (one each day) on a large menorah in the Western Wall Plaza.

Jewish leaders challenged Jesus at that feast to clearly declare if he really was the Messiah, the Anointed One. Jesus again reminded them that the miracles he did in his Father's name revealed who he was as God's Son. That infuriated them and they picked up stones to stone him to death for blasphemy. He slipped away from them.

Jesus returned to the Jordan River valley, where John had been baptizing. Large crowds came to hear him and believed in him. Later, after Martha and Mary sent him a message asking him to come and heal Lazarus, he returned to Bethany where he raised Lazarus from death. That news spread like wildfire. It infuriated the antagonistic Jewish leaders who then wanted both Jesus and Lazarus dead. From then on, they planned to kill Jesus. Caiaphas, the high priest, said that it was better for one man to die for the people than for the nation to be destroyed. [52]

Jesus withdrew to the hills around Ephraim. He continued to heal people, including ten lepers at the Samaritan border, who discovered their healing as they obeyed in faith and went to report to the priests. Only one of them, a Samaritan, gratefully returned to thank Jesus.

Later, Jesus journeyed to Jericho where he healed many including blind Bartimaeus, and he ate with the despised tax collector Zacchaeus. Crowds grew as he continued up the ranges toward Jerusalem. The crowds that followed Jesus expected that God's kingdom would come immediately through him.[53] It did, but not as they expected.

When Jesus and his disciples reached Bethany on the southern slopes of the Mount of Olives just east of Jerusalem, they often stayed there with Lazarus and his sisters Martha and Mary. The curious, adoring crowds continued to grow, wanting to see both Jesus and Lazarus. From there Jesus walked the mile into Jerusalem during his final week, usually returning to Bethany at night.

Religious leaders didn't want to kill Jesus during the Passover Feast as it might cause a riot among the people because Jesus was so popular, and many people were convinced he was their Messiah. Jesus, however, chose to give himself to them on the day that the Passover lambs were killed.

That day of preparation began at sundown when Jesus ate his final meal with his disciples. Then on that same Jewish day he

---

[52] John 10:41-42; 11:1-55.

[53] Luke 19:11.

prayed in Gethsemane, was arrested, endured the Jewish and Roman trials, the mocking and torture, and was crucified. He died around three that afternoon, the time that the Passover lambs were being slaughtered.

> **31** Since it was the day of Preparation, the Jews did not want the bodies left on the cross during the Sabbath, especially because that Sabbath was a day of great solemnity. So they asked Pilate to have the legs of the crucified men broken and the bodies removed. **32** Then the soldiers came and broke the legs of the first and of the other who had been crucified with him. **33** But when they came to Jesus and saw that he was already dead, they did not break his legs. **34** Instead, one of the soldiers pierced his side with a spear, and at once blood and water came out. **35** (He who saw this has testified so that you also may believe. His testimony is true, and he knows[g] that he tells the truth.) **36** These things occurred so that the scripture might be fulfilled, 'None of his bones shall be broken.' **37** And again another passage of scripture says, 'They will look on the one whom they have pierced.' ...
>
> **41** Now there was a garden in the place where he was crucified, and in the garden there was a new tomb in which no one had ever been laid. **42** And so, because it was the Jewish day of Preparation, and the tomb was nearby, they laid Jesus there. (John 19:31-37; 41-42)

The Passover was a special Sabbath which occurred on differing days of the week according to the calendar. Some scholars date the crucifixion of Jesus on Thursday 26 April 31 AD (daytime on 14th day of Nisan) followed by a "special Sabbath" for the Passover on Thursday night/Friday, 15th day of Nisan, then a regular weekly Sabbath on Friday night/Saturday, 16th day of Nisan, then the resurrection of Jesus on Sunday, 17th day of Nisan (the First Day of the Feast of First Fruits). That would also put the selection of the unblemished lamb for each household on Palm Sunday, 10th day of Nisan, when Jesus rode into Jerusalem as king.

See Appendix 4, Alternative Chronology, for more details.

5 PASSOVER TO PENTECOST

The week known as Holy Week or Passion Week, fills a third of each of the Gospels. It includes Jesus' triumphant entry into Jerusalem on Palm Sunday, cleansing the temple, debates and conflict with Jewish leaders, meals at Bethany, the Last Supper, agonizing prayer in Gethsemane, his trials by religious and political leaders, his flogging, crucifixion, burial and then his victorious resurrection on what we call Easter Sunday.

I give more detailed biblical descriptions of that week in my books *Crucified and Risen* and *The Lion of Judah,* with free PDFs on renewaljournal.com.

Although Jesus fulfilled many significant Scriptures in Holy Week, the Jewish scholars could not see it, and even his followers did not understand it until he explained it after his resurrection.

So the most momentous week in history unfolded as another week involving the annual Passover celebrations, with huge crowds filling Jerusalem. That final dramatic week in the crowded city, and areas surrounding Jerusalem, burst into open conflict with religious leaders and scholars. They criticized Jesus for allowing the noisy crowds to shout his praises.

Excited crowds cried out, "Hosanna," meaning, "Lord save us." They longed for a Messiah who would free them from Rome. The Roman garrison in the Antonia Fortress on the north side of the temple remained on high alert for any unrest or uprising, especially during the crowded feast days.

A very large crowd spread their cloaks on the road, and others cut branches from the trees and spread them on the road. ⁹ The crowds that went ahead of him and that followed were shouting,

> 'Hosanna to the Son of David!
> Blessed is the one who comes in the name of the Lord!
> Hosanna in the highest heaven!'

> ¹⁰ When he entered Jerusalem, the whole city was in turmoil, asking, 'Who is this?' ¹¹ The crowds were saying, 'This is the prophet Jesus from Nazareth in Galilee.'

> (Matthew 21:8-11 NIV; see Mark 11:1-10; Luke 19:28-40; John 12:12-19)

Jesus rode a donkey down the slopes of the Mount of Olives, across the Kidron brook, and to the temple area of the eastern side of the capital. He fulfilled a well-known prophecy from Zechariah 9:9 (Mt 21:5):

> Rejoice greatly, O daughter Zion!
> Shout aloud, O daughter Jerusalem!
> Lo, your king comes to you;
> triumphant and victorious is he,
> humble and riding on a donkey,
> on a colt, the foal of a donkey.

Jesus wept while everyone was rejoicing:

> As he came near and saw the city, he wept over it, saying, 'If you, even you, had only recognized on this day the things that make for peace! But now they are hidden from your eyes. Indeed, the days will come upon you,

when your enemies will set up ramparts around you and surround you, and hem you in on every side. They will crush you to the ground, you and your children within you, and they will not leave within you one stone upon another; because you did not recognize the time of your visitation from God.' (Luke 19:41-44)

Jesus saw its doom looming. About 40 years later in AD 70, Roman armies sacked the city, destroying its buildings and slaughtering its people.

Jesus immediately clashed with temple authorities by cleaning out the temple courts of unscrupulous merchants who raised huge incomes for the temple from the Passover crowds needing sacrificial animals.

Tensions with religious leaders simmered and exploded early that week as excited crowds heard Jesus teach, and he healed the blind and the crippled.

Each day early that week, Jesus taught in the temple area, consistently clashing with the religious hierarchy who tried to trap him, such as asking him about paying taxes to Rome. Jesus lifted the argument to declare the eternal values of God's kingdom.

Pharisees followed hundreds of laws and traditions based on Scripture, but Jesus summed up the commandments in two, to love God and love others. Sadducees courted political favour and denied life after death, angels, and demons, but Jesus reminded them that God is God of the living, including their ancestors who died.[54]

---

[54] Mark 12.

Jesus confounded religious scholars, showing the flaws in their beliefs, pointing out that their Scriptures spoke of him, but they could not see that. For example, the rejected stone discarded by the builders became the capstone or cornerstone, the most important stone of all.[55]

Jesus told a story of a vineyard owner sending his servants and then his only son to get his due portion but the tenants mistreated them and killed many including his son. The owner would severely punish them. Religious leaders realized that the story was aimed squarely at them.

At night Jesus and his closest disciples walked the mile to Bethany and ate with friends there. Those visits included a meal where Lazarus' sister Mary poured very expensive fragrant oil over him. Some disciples criticized her excess but Jesus praised her for her lavish love, which would be told throughout the world (as in Scripture and also here) and that she had prepared his body for burial.[56] That fragrance would stay on his body for many days.

To the rulers' delighted astonishment, one of Jesus' followers secretly agreed to betray Jesus to them quietly, away from the crowd. The rulers did not want to kill Jesus during the Passover feast to avoid a riot, but that is exactly when Jesus gave himself to them when Passover lambs were slain. That day began for Jews at sunset to the next sunset when Jesus' wounded, slaughtered body would lie in a new tomb nearby.

---

[55] Lk 20:17-18; Ps 118:22; Isa 28:16; Rom 9:33; 1 Peter 2:6.

[56] Matthew 26:6-13; Mark 14:3-9; John 12:1-8.

Before his arrest, torture, and execution, large crowds had excitedly welcomed him. But a few days later he was dead.

As I pondered this I realized it still happens. Millions trust him, believe in him, and follow him, but others reject him and his word. Many government authorities oppose him and his teaching, imprisoning and killing his followers. Many advocates of various religions kill his followers. Many media outlets attack his teaching and authority and condemn those who quote him. Many Christians criticize and attack other Christians who differ from them.

Good confronts evil. I realized that Jesus confronts and challenges us all because we all fall short of his standards and requirements. We must see our own failure and trust God for forgiveness and life. He gives eternal life.

That's why he chose to die for us, out of his great love for us all. He took our place. He took our guilt and sin upon himself and died in our place. He then rose victorious over death and now offers eternal life to all who trust in him.

The High Priest and the chief priests of the ruling Sanhedrin were determined to kill this dangerous, radical young man. Driven by jealousy of his popularity and the threat that his popularity may lead to a possible uprising and severe Roman retaliation, the religious leaders wanted him dead and this threat removed.

Eventually, they did have him killed. But Jesus gave himself to them knowing he would be publicly crucified when the Passover lambs were killed. Although the religious leaders did not want to kill Jesus during the feast and Pilate did not want to kill Jesus at all, Jesus chose to die during the feast on the Preparation Day when the sacrificial Pascal Lambs were slain, the day before the special Passover Sabbath.[57] He himself is the eternal Lamb of God who takes away our sin.

Jesus ate the Passover, the Last Supper, on the same Jewish day that he died. He ate his Passover meal with his closest disciples knowing it would be his last meal with them before his death the next afternoon. He would fulfil the meaning of the Passover as the unblemished Lamb of God, slain for us all.

He gave that meal new meaning. We call it the Last Supper. He told them the bread was his body and the wine was his blood. He fulfilled its meaning and significance. He was giving his perfect body as a sacrifice for us all. He told them to remember him each time they did that. It includes what we now call communion or the Eucharist (Thanksgiving) and can be part of our eating and drinking together in our homes as it was in the early church.

The disciples didn't realize the significance of that meal and even argued about who among them was the greatest. Jesus silenced that discussion by washing their feet, dressed like a servant with a towel around his waist which he used to wipe their feet. That confronted them. Peter objected, but Jesus told him he must accept it and that the greatest was a servant and they must follow his example and love and serve one another.[58]

Jesus shared his heart with his closest friends there and prayed for them. He promised that he would always be with them by his Spirit in them.[59]

---

[57] Mark 15:42; Luke 23:54; John 18:28; 19:14, 31, 42; and Matthew 27:62.

[58] Luke 22:24-27; John 13:1-17.

[59] John 13-17.

That meal ended with singing a psalm. Traditionally the Passover meal concluded with singing one of the Hillel psalms of praise, Psalms 115-118. Perhaps they sang the salvation song, Psalm 115, so full of prophecies that Jesus would fulfil.

> ⁹ O Israel, trust in the LORD!
> He is their help and their shield.
> ¹⁰ O house of Aaron, trust in the LORD!
> He is their help and their shield.
> ¹¹ You who fear the LORD, trust in the LORD!
> He is their help and their shield.
>
> ¹² The LORD has been mindful of us; he will bless us;
> he will bless the house of Israel;
> he will bless the house of Aaron;
> ¹³ he will bless those who fear the LORD,
> both small and great.
>
> ¹⁴ May the LORD give you increase,
> both you and your children.
> ¹⁵ May you be blessed by the LORD,
> who made heaven and earth.
>
> ¹⁶ The heavens are the LORD's heavens,
> but the earth he has given to human beings.
> ¹⁷ The dead do not praise the LORD,
> nor do any that go down into silence.
> ¹⁸ But we will bless the LORD
> from this time on and forevermore.
> Praise the LORD!
> (Psalm 115:9-18)

During that meal, Jesus had sent Judas to do what Judas had already planned to do, betray him to the priests. Following their meal the group went out with Jesus past the temple, across the

Kidron brook to the Olive Grove of Gethsemane on the lower slopes of the Mount of Olives just east of the city.

There in the Garden or Grove of Gethsemane Jesus prayed three times alone in agony. His exhausted disciples fell asleep. Jesus' sweat was infused with blood. He asked his Father if this cup could pass from him, but added, "Not my will but yours be done." A little later, when Peter fought the mob, Jesus stopped him, saying that he must drink the cup his Father gave him.

Some scholars see his prayer in Gethsemane as a prayer to be delivered from premature death. The letter to the Hebrews describes that possibility this way:

> [7] In the days of his flesh, Jesus offered up prayers and supplications, with loud cries and tears, to the one who was able to save him from death, and he was heard because of his reverent submission. [8] Although he was a Son, he learned obedience through what he suffered; [9] and having been made perfect, he became the source of eternal salvation for all who obey him, [10] having been designated by God a high priest according to the order of Melchizedek. (Hebrews 5:7-10)

Judas led a mob there armed with weapons to arrest Jesus who surrendered himself to them. The mob fell backwards at Jesus' awesome presence. Peter sliced the ear of Malchus the high priest's servant but Jesus rebuked Peter and healed the ear, his last healing act showing his love for his enemies.

The Trials

Jesus endured three religious and three civil trials, including two beatings and more personal abuse, leaving him savagely wounded and weakened so much that, strong as he was, he could not carry the crossbeam to his execution as other prisoners did. This summary describes some of those tense, rushed events including the hurried and illegal late-night to early-morning meeting of the partial Sanhedrin, the executive council of the priests. The Sanhedrin of 70 priests collaborated with Rome and was accountable to Roman officials. Annas, a former high priest, and his son-in-law Caiaphas, the current high priest, were part of the influential Sadducee priestly families acceptable to and appointed by Roman officials.

(1) Trial with Annas, father-in-law of the high priest

Soldiers of the temple guard arrested Jesus in Gethsemane late at night and bound him. They took him first to Annas, who quizzed Jesus about his disciples and his teaching. Jesus reminded Annas that he had spoken freely and openly, not secretly, and that Annas could ask those who heard him. A soldier of the temple guard, shocked by that answer, struck Jesus' face, earning a rebuke from Jesus who had said nothing wrong. The rough, hostile treatment of Jesus had begun. Annas then sent the bound Jesus to Caiaphas (John 18:12-14, 19-24).

(2) Trial with Caiaphas, the high priest

After that initial interrogation, they took Jesus to be judged by Caiaphas, the high priest, with a small group of angry elders involved all night from the arrest in Gethsemane.

Two of Jesus' followers were there. One of them, known to the High Priest (possibly Nicodemus who had supported Jesus in the Sanhedrin, or the story's author), arranged for Peter to come in. Peter had followed at a distance and later he warmed himself at the charcoal fire in the high priest's courtyard until he was challenged there and denied knowing Jesus (John 18:10-11, 14; Luke 22:49-62). Jesus turned and looked at Peter who then remembered how Jesus had told him that Peter would deny Jesus three times before the rooster crowed twice. At the rooster's second crowing Peter went away and wept bitterly (Luke 22:61-62).

Many chief priests, elders, and scribes had been hastily assembled. Jesus remained silent as witnesses argued and disagreed about what he had said. Finally, Caiaphas asked Jesus if he was the Messiah, the Son of God, and Jesus affirmed his statement. They saw that as blasphemy and the high priest tore his own robes in rage. They condemned Jesus as worthy of death. They spat on him, blindfolded him, and struck him asking him to prophecy and say who did it. The guards then took him and severely beat him (Mark 14:53-65).

A medical doctor described the two floggings this way:

> Jesus' beatings were particularly severe, beyond what a condemned prisoner would ordinarily experience. Jesus was beaten by Jewish Temple Guard soldiers prior to being placed into Roman custody. He was then again beaten and scourged by Roman soldiers. The "whole

cohort" of Roman soldiers participated in mocking and severely beating him. He was severely flogged, spit on, blindfolded, and hit with a rod used as a mock royal scepter (Matt. 27: 27-31, John 19: 1-3).

The severity of Jesus' initial beatings while in Jewish custody should not be overlooked. Thomas McGovern, M.D., makes an interesting observation about Luke's description of Jesus' first beating while in Jewish custody. "Now the men who were holding Jesus under guard began to mock him and beat him." (Luke 22: 63). Luke uses the Greek verb *derontes* (δέροντες) for the phrase "and beat him." The Greek root of this word is the same for skin, *derma* (δέρμα), and carries the primary meaning of "to flay the skin." "To beat" is a secondary meaning. When the word is used to describe a beating or whipping, it implies a heightened severity of thrashing and cudgeling. Luke as a physician seems to use specific language to precisely describe the severity of Jesus' beating.

Since the Sanhedrin would have executed Jesus if they had the opportunity to do so, it seems likely that his beating from the Temple Guard would have been particularly severe. The maximum penalty short of death by Jewish law was forty stripes (Deut. 25: 3). Jewish courts had autonomy in corporal punishment and could lash offenders at their discretion without Roman interference. Roman soldiers were free to beat condemned prisoners without restriction, the only stipulation being that the prisoner should not be beaten to death prior to crucifixion.

Accordingly, it is traditionally held that Jesus was scourged twice. The first beating was in the home of Caiaphas the High Priest, the second by Roman soldiers under order of Pontius Pilate.

[Bergeron, Joseph W. *The Crucifixion of Jesus*: A Medical Doctor Examines the Death and Resurrection of Christ. St. Polycarp Publishing House. Chapter 6: The execution of Jesus.]

(3) Trial with the Sanhedrin

By dawn the chief priests had consulted elders, scribes, and the council, a partial group of the 70-member Sanhedrin, which had the authority to pass judgment. They had asked Jesus if he was the Messiah, the Son of God, and he affirmed their words. Furiously, they condemned him to death. Joseph from Arimathea was one of the few council members who disagreed with their judgment.

Previously, in a heated Sanhedrin debate, Caiaphas had advised them that it was better to have one person die for the people than for Rome to attack and destroy the nation (John 11:45-53; Luke 22:63-71; 23:1, 50-51).

(4) Trial with Pilate, the Governor

The council bound Jesus and took him to Pilate, the Governor because they did not have the authority to execute him (Mark 15:1).

Seized with remorse at this development, Judas flung back his 30 pieces of silver that the priests had given him to betray Jesus, and he went out and hanged himself (Matthew 27:1-10).

Pilate came out to meet the angry assembly. They accused Jesus of perverting the nation, forbidding people to pay taxes, and declaring himself the Messiah, a king. Pilate asked Jesus if he really was the king of the Jews, and Jesus affirmed his statement.

Pilate concluded from his interrogation that Jesus had done nothing worthy of death. But the priests insisted that Jesus was dangerous and had stirred up the people by his teaching in the province of Judea beginning from Galilee (Luke 23:1-5). Their reference to Galilee gave Pilate a way out, so he sent Jesus to Herod, the ruler in Galilee, for judgement.

(5) Trial with Herod Antipas

Herod Antipas, the tetrarch of Galilee, was in Jerusalem for the feast. Herod had wanted to see Jesus for a long time and he hoped to see him do some miracle. He questioned Jesus at length but Jesus said nothing. The chief priests and scribes accused him vehemently. Herod and his soldiers mocked Jesus and put an elegant robe on him to send him back to Pilate. That day Herod and Pilate, who had been enemies, became friends (Luke 23:6-12).

Previously Herod had beheaded John the Baptist and he had wanted to kill Jesus also (Luke 13:31-33) but Jesus had told the religious leaders to tell that fox that he, Jesus, would finish his work and then go to Jerusalem. Now in Jerusalem, Herod finally met him but treated him with contempt. So the frustrated, angry group of his accusers, with the temple guard, returned their prisoner to the governor.

(6) Second Trial with Pilate

Pilate wanted to release Jesus but the fanatical religious leaders strenuously opposed it. They did not enter the governor's fortress palace because they would have been ritually defiled and they wanted to eat the Passover meal that night.

Pilate went out to them and told them to judge Jesus by their own law but they objected loudly because they wanted him crucified. Then Pilate entered his headquarters again and interrogated Jesus further about his kingdom. Pilate's wife sent him a message warning him to have nothing to do with that victim because she had had a bad dream about him.

Then Pilate tried another ploy. Each year at their Passover festival he offered to release a prisoner. He offered them the choice of a notorious prisoner named Jesus Barabbas or their victim Jesus Christ. The chief priests and elders persuaded the crowd to shout for Barabbas and to have Jesus killed. A riot was beginning so Pilate gave in, washed his hands of the whole thing, and handed Jesus over to the soldiers to be flogged and crucified (Matthew 27:15-26).

Many people are familiar with the flogging or scourging of Jesus by the Roman soldiers. That was normal practice for victims before the crucifixion. The film *The Passion* graphically portrays Roman scourging, although even that depiction does not show the full horror of the scourging from head to foot of the victim, as can be seen in the image of a crucified man on the Shroud of Turin, savagely whipped and wounded from shoulders to feet.

A Jewish flogging was limited to 40 lashes (Deuteronomy 25:3), but Roman soldiers had no limit except that the victim should survive the flogging before being crucified. Roman soldiers scourged with a flagellum, a whip of leather strips with pieces of lead or bone sewn into the ends. They scourged the entire body. Jesus' flogging would have been brutal because he was being executed as the king of the Jews and would be regarded by the Roman soldiers as a rebel defying their Roman Empire.

The governor's soldiers then took Jesus into the headquarters and gathered the whole Jerusalem cohort, normally 480 soldiers. They stripped him, put a scarlet robe on him, shoved a crown of thorns on his head, put a reed in his right hand, and knelt down, mocking him. They spat on him and struck him on the head. After they mocked him they put his own clothes on him and took him out to crucify him (Matthew 27:27-31).

(7) Trial in heaven

In addition to the rushed human trials, I want to include the ultimate, eternal verdict of heaven by the Judge of the whole earth. The courts of heaven declared Jesus to be the pure, perfect offering, the one and only substitute for our sin. God accepted the sacrifice of his Son in our place, our Redeemer, our Saviour, and our Lord. Paul wrote, "For our sake he made him to be sin who knew no sin so that in him we might become the righteousness of God." (2 Corinthians 5:21)

Isaiah's servant song declared it:

> Surely he has borne our infirmities
> and carried our diseases;
> yet we accounted him stricken,
> struck down by God, and afflicted.
> 5 But he was wounded for our transgressions,
> crushed for our iniquities;
> upon him was the punishment that made us whole,
> and by his bruises, we are healed.

> **6** All we like sheep have gone astray;
> we have all turned to our own way,
> and the LORD has laid on him
> the iniquity of us all. (Isaiah 53:4-6)

The hosts of heaven declared it:

> Then I looked, and I heard the voice of many angels around the throne, the living creatures, and the elders; and the number of them was ten thousand times ten thousand, and thousands of thousands, saying with a loud voice:

> "Worthy is the Lamb who was slain
> To receive power and riches and wisdom,
> And strength and honour and glory and blessing!"
> (Revelation 5:11 NKJV)

Crucifixion

Romans ruled forcefully with an iron rod. They crucified thousands of rebellious slaves and criminals, such as 6,000 crucified in the Spartacus rebellion of 70 BC, and 500 people a day in the Jewish rebellion of AD 70. Roman citizens were exempt from the degrading punishment of crucifixion. The Romans used crucifixion for six centuries until Emperor Constantine outlawed it around AD 313.

The conquering Romans made sure their victims suffered maximum agony and humiliation on thousands of crosses, suffering publicly and slowly in excruciating pain to their last agonized breath. That's how we got our English words *excruciate* (ex-crux - out of the cross) and *agony* from the Greek word *agon* (struggle or contest).

Roman soldiers could torture and mock their hapless victims before they crucified them. Jesus was brutally scourged, mocked, reviled, and then crucified. Previously strong and healthy, he suffered excruciating pain, shock, and weakness. He did not have enough strength to carry the crossbeam as the other victims did. He had been more brutally tortured than usual.

The three victims that day each carried their crossbeam (*patibulum*) to the place of public execution. Jesus was then too weak to do that, so the soldiers forced Simon of Cyrene, coming in from the country, to carry it. The cross in Scripture can mean both the crossbeam and the whole gruesome structure. Most common was the Tau structure, like a capital T. Victims were nailed to the crossbeam and hoisted onto the tree trunk or stake and their feet nailed to it. An artistic invention is the block of wood attached to the front of the cross to support feet but Roman soldiers did not add it. Another symbolic artistic invention is the crown of thorns on Jesus' head on the cross. Thorns were used in the prior torture, and then Jesus' clothes were put back on him until removed again at the crucifixion.

Usually, four soldiers would crucify each victim supervised by a centurion. That day they crucified three with Jesus in the middle. Romans crucified their victims along the main road just outside a town or village where it could be seen. They lopped trees and their victims carried the crossbeam to the dreadful execution site where they were nailed to the crossbar and hoisted onto a tree, a tree trunk, or a stake. Peter later wrote that he bore our sins in his own body on the tree.[60] The execution site just outside Jerusalem's city wall was called the place of the skull

---

[60] 1 Peter 2:24; also Acts 10:39; 13:29.

with graves nearby. There are tombs and graves just outside the Old City wall even today.

Spectators taunted the central victim who had a sign above him declaring in Aramaic, Greek, and Latin that he was the king of the Jews. The soldiers divided their victims' clothes among themselves and gambled for Jesus' tunic because it was woven as one whole garment. Religious leaders and soldiers scoffed at him as a Messiah and king who couldn't save himself or others.[61]

They didn't know that by this very sacrifice of his perfect life, he would save all who trust in him.

He was crucified about nine o'clock, and darkness came over the land from noon. The Lamb of God died around three o'clock, the time the unblemished Paschal Lambs were being slain in the temple that afternoon.

Eye-witnesses saw and heard the horrendous spectacle. John saw it. He was there with faithful women including Jesus' mother Mary, her sister (usually identified as Salome, John's mother), Mary the wife of Clopas, and Mary Magdalene.[62]

This crucifixion account follows the traditional sequence of the statements that Jesus made while dying during six agonizing hours, including quoting Psalms 22:1 and 31:5.

---

[61] Luke 23:35-37.

[62] Matthew 27:55-56; Mark 15:40-41; Luke 23:49.

1. *Father forgive them, for they know not what they do.*

As they crucified him Jesus said, "Father, forgive them; for they do not know what they are doing" (Luke 23:34). He continued to demonstrate love and forgiveness.

2. *Truly, I say to you, today you will be with me in paradise.*

One of the criminals kept on deriding Jesus but the other criminal rebuked him and believed in Jesus, pleading, "Jesus, remember me when you come into your kingdom." Jesus replied, "Truly I tell you, today you will be with me in Paradise" (Luke 23:43). That was a very public conversion moment for a guilty man seeking life. God's love, grace, mercy, and forgiveness are available to us all as Jesus demonstrated even while dying – especially by dying.

3. *Woman, behold your son; behold your mother.*

When Jesus saw his mother and the disciple he loved standing with her, he said to his mother in Aramaic, "Dear woman, here is your son" and said to the disciple, "Here is your mother" (John 19:26-27). That disciple, the author of the story, usually identified as John, took Mary to his home.

4. *My God, My God, why have you forsaken me?*

Darkness covered the land from noon to three in the afternoon, the time when Passover lambs were being slaughtered. Jesus loudly quoted the start of a messianic Psalm: "Eli, Eli, lema sabachthani?" - "My God, my God, why have you forsaken me?"

That Psalm continues: "All those who see Me ridicule Me; They shoot out the lip, they shake the head, saying, 'He trusted in the Lord, let Him rescue Him; Let Him deliver Him' ... They pierced My hands and My feet ...They look and stare at Me. They divide My garments among them, and for My clothing they cast lots." Some people thought he was calling for Elijah. (Matthew 27:45-49; Mark 15:34; Psalm 22:1, 7-8, 16-18) Jesus quoted that messianic psalm as he literally fulfilled it on the cross.

5. *I thirst.*

At the excruciating end of his life, Jesus gasped, "I am thirsty" (John 19:28). A jar of sour wine was nearby so someone put a sponge full of the wine on a branch of hyssop and held it to his mouth (John 19:28-29; Psalm 22:15; 69:3,21). It's interesting that Israelites used hyssop to put blood on their doorways at their first Passover in Egypt.

6. *It is finished.*

When Jesus knew that all he had come to do had been done, he received the wine, and he said, "It is finished." That can be translated as, "It is accomplished." (John 19:30)

7. *Father, into your hands I commit my spirit.*

Jesus cried out with a loud voice, "Father, into your hands I commit my spirit" (Luke 23:46; Psalm 31:5), and breathed his last, quoting Scripture. The greatest loving sacrifice in all of history was done.

The supervising centurion declared that the central victim was indeed innocent and was God's Son.

Here is a summary of those words from the cross.

1 Father forgive them, for they know not what they do.
(Luke 23:34)

2 Truly, I say to you, today you will be with me in paradise. (Luke 23:43)

3 Woman, behold your son; behold your mother. (John 19:26-27)

4 My God, My God, why have you forsaken me? (Matthew 27:46; Mark 15:34; Ps 22:1)[63]

5 I thirst. (John 19:28; Psalm 21:15-16; 69:21)

6 It is finished. (John 19:30)

7 Father, into your hands I commit my spirit. (Luke 23:46; Psalm 31:5)

Traditionally, these seven statements are called words of

1. Forgiveness,

2. Salvation,

3. Relationship,

4. Abandonment,

5. Distress,

6. Triumph, and

7. Reunion.

Eventually, the soldiers smashed the legs of the two victims still alive so they died quickly, no longer able to push up from their spiked feet to gasp more breath. Religious leaders wanted them

---

[63] The Aramaic can be translated "For this purpose you have spared me." (The Passion Translation)

off the crosses before the Passover Sabbath began at sunset. The central victim was already dead so a soldier pierced his side and heart with a spear to be sure. Blood and water gushed out.

The mystery deepened rapidly. Matthew reported that the thick curtain in the temple was split from top to bottom. The earth shook, rocks split and tombs broke open. The bodies of many holy people who had died were raised to life and came out of the tombs after Jesus' resurrection and went into the city and appeared to many people.[64]

The prophet Isaiah foretold the extreme suffering of the Messiah in his Servant Songs.[65] The last of those songs graphically describes the suffering of God's Servant, ultimately fulfilled in Jesus.

> Who has believed what we have heard?
> And to whom has the arm of the LORD been revealed?
> 2 For he grew up before him like a young plant,
> and like a root out of dry ground;
> he had no form or majesty that we should look at him,
> nothing in his appearance that we should desire him.
> 3 He was despised and rejected by others;
> a man of suffering and acquainted with infirmity;
> and as one from whom others hide their faces
> he was despised, and we held him of no account.
>
> 4 Surely he has borne our infirmities
> and carried our diseases;
> yet we accounted him stricken,

---

64 Matthew 27:51-52.

65 Isaiah 42:1-4; 49:1-6; 50:4-9; 52:13-53:12.

struck down by God, and afflicted.
5 But he was wounded for our transgressions,
crushed for our iniquities;
upon him was the punishment that made us whole,
and by his bruises we are healed.
6 All we like sheep have gone astray;
we have all turned to our own way,
and the **Lord** has laid on him
the iniquity of us all.

7 He was oppressed, and he was afflicted,
yet he did not open his mouth;
like a lamb that is led to the slaughter,
and like a sheep that before its shearers is silent,
so he did not open his mouth.
8 By a perversion of justice he was taken away.
Who could have imagined his future?
For he was cut off from the land of the living,
stricken for the transgression of my people.
9 They made his grave with the wicked
and his tomb with the rich,
although he had done no violence,
and there was no deceit in his mouth.

10 Yet it was the will of the *Lord* to crush him with pain.
When you make his life an offering for sin,
he shall see his offspring, and shall prolong his days;
through him the will of the *Lord* shall prosper.
11 Out of his anguish he shall see light;
he shall find satisfaction through his knowledge.
The righteous one, my servant, shall make many
righteous,
and he shall bear their iniquities.

12 Therefore I will allot him a portion with the great,
and he shall divide the spoil with the strong;
because he poured out himself to death,
and was numbered with the transgressors;
yet he bore the sin of many,
and made intercession for the transgressors. (Isaiah
53:1-12)

I tell events in this book in more detail in my book *The Lion of Judah*, with a free PDF on renewaljournal.com. There I include extra passages including some from Paul's letters and from various passages in the New Testament including The Revelation. Matthew and John witnessed these events personally. Mark may have seen some of it in Jerusalem. Luke gathered his reports from eyewitnesses for his two books, the *Gospel of Luke* and *The Acts of the Apostles*.

Joseph of Arimathea, assisted by Nicodemus, received permission to take Jesus' body from the cross and placed the body in his new tomb nearby. He wrapped Jesus' body in a large linen sheet with a cloth around his head. He had a huge stone rolled in front of the tomb. The next day the chief priests received permission to seal the stone and keep a guard of soldiers on watch to prevent anyone from stealing the body.

Resurrection

Rumours began to spread that Passover weekend.

Most people thought that the unbelievable rumours were impossible, and said so.

Only a few, very few at first, thought the crucified Messiah was alive. A month later some of his followers still doubted that it had happened and that he really was alive.[66]

Crucified, as thousands were, their Messiah and King then appeared mysteriously during 40 days from the full moon at Passover until his ascension beyond the clouds.

On the third day, he mysteriously appeared to many of his friends. That day and evening he explained to them how the Scriptures said that the Messiah had to suffer.

These mysterious events transformed the lives of the people involved and shaped the history of the world. This story covers the most momentous events in history because it not only affected those involved then but also changed the lives and eternal destinies of countless millions throughout history.

This chapter includes a brief overview of those resurrection appearances.

Resurrection Sunday

(1) Mary Magdalene - Mark 16:9; John 20:11-18

(2) The Women - Matthew 28:9-10

---

[66] Matthew 28:17.

(3) Cleopas and friend, Emmaus Road – Mark 16:12-13; Luke 24:13-34

(4) Simon Peter - Luke 24:34; 1 Corinthians 15:5

(5) The Disciples - Mark 16:14; Luke 24:36-49; John 20:19-23; 1 Corinthians 15:5

(1) Mary Magdalene

After the Passover Sabbath, Mary, her sister (usually identified as Salome), and Mary Magdalene went to the tomb at dawn and found the large stone rolled away and the body gone. An angel in the tomb told them that Jesus was alive: "He is risen, as he said."

The angel sent the women to tell the others, so Mary Magdalene rushed back and told Peter and John who ran to the tomb but found it empty with the linen cloth there and the head cloth folded near it.

Mary Magdalene stayed on at the tomb, weeping. She looked inside the tomb and saw two angels who asked her why she was weeping. Then she saw a man she thought was the gardener, who also asked her why she was weeping, so she asked him if he had moved the body. Jesus said, "Mary."

Astonished, she cried out in Aramaic, 'Rabboni!' (Which means 'Teacher'). Jesus also told her to go and tell the news to the others.

(2) The Women

The women later reported that there had been an earthquake and a large angel had rolled away the stone. The guards were terrified and became like dead men.

Angels appear often in Scripture, usually as strong young men, never with wings. Cherubim and seraphim and some heavenly creatures are winged.

Jesus appeared to the women after they had seen the angel at the tomb and were rushing back. He instructed them to tell the others and he would see them also in Galilee.

(3) Cleopas and Friend on the Emmaus Road

That same day, Cleopas and his friend walked about seven miles to Emmaus. Jesus joined them as they walked but they did not recognize him and they told him about the crucifixion and the strange events of that morning. Jesus reminded them from the Law and all the Prophets that the Messiah had to suffer and then enter his glory. They invited him for a meal and as he gave thanks they realized who he was, but he disappeared. Immediately they ran back to Jerusalem to tell the others.

(4) Simon Peter

Cleopas and his friend found the disciples and others gathered together. The disciples said the news was all true, and that Jesus had also appeared that day to Simon Peter.

(5) The Disciples behind locked doors

That evening as the disciples met behind locked doors Jesus appeared to them. At first, they were startled and afraid, thinking he was a ghost. He said, "Shalom" and showed them his hands and side and invited them to touch him and see he really was alive. He ate their cooked fish with them. They were overjoyed. He reminded them that he had previously told them that what was written about him in the Law, the Prophets, and the Psalms, had to be fulfilled and that repentance and forgiveness would be preached in his name to all nations.

He breathed on them saying, "Receive the Holy Spirit." He told them he would send them what his Father had promised but that they should wait until they were clothed with power from on high.

40 Days (Acts 1:3)

(6) Disciples with Thomas, one week later - John 20:24-29.

(7) 500 at once - 1 Corinthians 15:6.

(8) James - 1 Corinthians 15:7.

(9) Galilee Shore - John 21:1-25.

(10) Galilee Mountain - Matthew 28:16-20.

(11) Eating with the disciples – Acts 1:4-5.

(12) Ascension - Mount of Olives - Luke 24:50-51; Acts 1:6-9.

(6) The Disciples with Thomas, one week later

Thomas missed that first night did not believe it and would not believe unless he could touch Jesus' wounds. A week later they all met again. Though the doors were locked, Jesus came and said, "Shalom." He invited Thomas to touch his hands and side and to stop doubting and to believe. Thomas said, "My Lord and my God!" Jesus said, "Because you have seen me, you have believed; blessed are those who have not seen and yet have believed." (John 20:24-29)

(7) 500 at once

Paul later reported, "After that, he appeared to more than five hundred of the brothers and sisters at the same time, most of whom are still living, though some have fallen asleep."

(8) James (and Paul's vision)

Paul also reported, "Then he appeared to James, then to all the apostles, and last of all he appeared to me also, as to one abnormally born." James, the brother of Jesus became a key leader in the church of Jerusalem and wrote a pastoral letter now included in Scripture.

(9) Galilee Shore

Afterwards Jesus appeared to seven of his disciples, by the Sea of Galilee. Simon Peter, Thomas, Nathanael, James and John, and two other disciples had been fishing unsuccessfully all night. Early in the morning Jesus stood on the shore and told them to throw their net on the right side of the boat. When they did, they couldn't haul in the net because of the large catch.

John said "It is the Lord!" and Peter grabbed his cloak and swam about 100m to the shore. The others followed in the boat, towing the net full of fish. At the shore, they saw a fire of burning coals there with fish on it and some bread. Jesus told them to get some of their fish. They discovered they had 153 large fish but even with so many the net was not torn. They all ate together.

When they had finished Jesus asked Peter three times if Peter loved him and Peter said he did. Peter was hurt when Jesus asked him the third time. Each time Jesus commissioned Peter to feed his sheep or lambs. Jesus said that when Peter was old he would stretch out his hands and others would dress him and take him where he did not want to go, indicating how Peter would die. Tradition says Peter was crucified in Rome and asked to be crucified upside down because he was not worthy to die as Jesus did. A rumour spread that John would not die but Jesus did not say that. When Peter asked about John, Jesus said, "If I want him to remain alive until I return, what is that to you?'

(10) Galilee Mountain: The Great Commission

When eleven disciples met Jesus on a mountain in Galilee, even though some doubted, Jesus gave them what we call the Great Commission:

> All authority in heaven and on earth has been given to me. Therefore go and make disciples of all nations, baptizing them in the name of the Father and of the Son and of the Holy Spirit, and teaching them to obey everything I have commanded you. And surely I am with you always, to the very end of the age.' (Matthew 28:16-20)

(11) Eating with disciples

Jesus met with his disciples many times during those 40 days, and one time while they ate together in Jerusalem, he told them to wait there until God's power came upon them.

> While staying with them, he ordered them not to leave Jerusalem, but to wait there for the promise of the Father. 'This', he said, 'is what you have heard from me; for John baptized with water, but you will be baptized with the Holy Spirit not many days from now.' (Acts 1:4-5)

(12) Ascension

Jesus took his disciples out to the vicinity of Bethany on the Mount of Olives and blessed them. While he was blessing them, he left them and was taken up into heaven. There, on that mountain overlooking Jerusalem, he told them they would not know the times or dates the Father had set but he gave them his final promise:

> But you will receive power when the Holy Spirit comes on you; and you will be my witnesses in Jerusalem, and in all Judea and Samaria, and to the ends of the earth. (Acts 1:8)

Then he ascended and a cloud hid him from their sight. While they looked up intently, two men in white stood beside them and told them that this same Jesus would come back in the same way they saw him go into heaven.

Jesus' promise about the Holy Spirit was dramatically fulfilled ten days later at Pentecost. They were filled with the Holy Spirit and when Peter preached boldly that day around 3,000 people believed. The church grew rapidly.

Believers met in homes and also worshipped in the temple until persecution drove many of them out of Jerusalem. Stephen, the first of many martyrs, was stoned to death near the temple, just outside the city wall. Everywhere they went they told the good news of Jesus, God's Son, and multitudes believed.

They prayed for new believers to be filled with God's Spirit. Philip preached and prayed powerfully for large numbers in Samaria, and then Peter and John came and laid hands on the believers and the Holy Spirit came upon them also. Samaritans were included among the believers.

Saul had been persecuting believers, but a bright light blinded him, and he heard Jesus speak to him on the road to Damascus in Syria, where he was headed to persecute more believers. One of those believers, Ananias, prayed for Saul who was then healed and filled with the Spirit. He quickly became an effective evangelist and missionary, renamed Paul, known as an apostle to the Gentiles.

Peter eventually broke strict traditions and preached in the home of the centurion Cornelius. His whole household believed and God's Spirit was poured out on them while Peter was preaching to them. The good news kept spreading through the Roman Empire.

Those Spirit-filled believers learned to command healing and cast out evil spirits in Jesus' name. Believers were first called Christians, Christ-followers, in the multi-national, multi-racial church at Antioch in Syria.

Some believers had visions of Jesus or of angels as Paul did, or as John did when imprisoned on Patmos. John recorded those visions for us in the book of The Revelation of Jesus Christ, now the last book in the Bible. It includes these inspiring revelations:

> Then I turned to see whose voice it was that spoke to me, and on turning I saw seven golden lampstands, 13 and in the midst of the lampstands I saw one like the Son of Man, clothed with a long robe and with a golden sash across his chest. 14 His head and his hair were white as white wool, white as snow; his eyes were like a flame of fire, 15 his feet were like burnished bronze, refined as in a furnace, and his voice was like the sound of many waters. 16 In his right hand he held seven stars, and from his mouth came a sharp, two-edged sword, and his face was like the sun shining with full force.
>
> 17 When I saw him, I fell at his feet as though dead. But he placed his right hand on me, saying, 'Do not be afraid; I am the first and the last, 18 and the living one. I was dead,

and see, I am alive forever and ever, and I have the keys of Death and of Hades. (Revelation 1:12-18)

Then I saw heaven opened, and there was a white horse! Its rider is called Faithful and True, and in righteousness, he judges and makes war. 12 His eyes are like a flame of fire, and on his head are many diadems; and he has a name inscribed that no one knows but himself. 13 He is clothed in a robe dipped in blood, and his name is called The Word of God. 14 And the armies of heaven, wearing fine linen, white and pure, were following him on white horses. 15 From his mouth comes a sharp sword with which to strike down the nations, and he will rule them with a rod of iron; he will tread the wine press of the fury of the wrath of God the Almighty. 16 On his robe and on his thigh he has a name inscribed, 'King of kings and Lord of lords'. (Revelation 19:11-16)

And the one who was seated on the throne said, 'See, I am making all things new.' Also, he said, 'Write this, for these words are trustworthy and true.' 6 Then he said to me, 'It is done! I am the Alpha and the Omega, the beginning and the end. To the thirsty, I will give water as a gift from the spring of the water of life. 7 Those who conquer will inherit these things, and I will be their God and they will be my children. (Revelation 21:5-7)

'It is I, Jesus, who sent my angel to you with this testimony for the churches. I am the root and the descendant of David, the bright morning star.'

The Spirit and the bride say, 'Come.'
And let everyone who hears say, 'Come.'
And let everyone who is thirsty come.

Let anyone who wishes take the water of life as a gift. (Revelation 22:16-17)

CONCLUSION

The amazing life of Jesus is history's great love story. The overview in this brief book points you to the great good news of who Jesus is and what he did. That story is told best in the Bible, God's inspired word.

I hope this brief commentary points you again to that God-breathed living word. It gave me fresh insights as I researched the harmonized story of these gospels.

Many writers discuss the popular five love languages: affirmation, service, gifts, time, and touch. Jesus demonstrated all these in various ways.

He affirmed and admired faith, especially faith in him for healing and help. He served daily and showed it dramatically by washing his disciples' feet. He gave his life for us and ultimately he gives eternal life to all who believe. His three years of quality time with his followers prepared them to serve. His touch brought physical and spiritual healing and freedom to multitudes.

I love the way John summed up the reason for writing his Gospel: "Now Jesus did many other signs in the presence of his disciples, which are not written in this book. But these are written so that you may come to believe that Jesus is the Messiah, the Son of God, and that through believing you may have life in his name." (John 20:31)

That is my prayer for you, my reader. Here is my echoing sonnet, penned over fifty years ago.

Sin stalks the soul, and permeates the whole

Of life lived here where we, while bound by fear,

Hunt far and near for freedom to appear

From pole to pole with our minds in control.

That worthy goal seems mockery. Sin stole

Our freedom dear, left pain and woe to sear

Each life, a mere heartache, or sob, or tear,

Like a lost mole, blind, dirty in its hole.

God's love stepped in to fight and conquer sin

Through Christ who bled and died and rose as Head

Supreme of all who claim Him Lord. Our fall,

Clamour and din may end in Him. We win

Release from dread, freedom, life from the dead,

Unbound from gall, in answer to His call.

DISCUSSION QUESTIONS

Chapter 1: Birth and Boyhood

1. What is one of your favourite Christmas carols and why?

2. What surprises you most about the Christmas story?

3. What challenges you about the boyhood and youth of Jesus?

What would you like people to pray about for you?

Chapter 2: Ministry Begins

1. Why do you think Jesus' public ministry began after his baptism?

2. What puzzles you most about Jesus' ministry? (e.g. casting out spirits)

3. What challenges you about being a disciple of Jesus?

What prayer would you appreciate receiving?

Chapter 3: First to Second Passovers

1. Why do you think John 3:16 is so popular and well-known?

2. Who can you identify with in Jesus' early ministry? (e.g. Nicodemus, Samaritan woman, disciples, religious leaders)

3. What do you think challenged Jesus' disciples?

What prayer would encourage you just now?

Chapter 4: Second to Third Passovers

1. What impresses you most about Jesus?

2. What challenges you most about Jesus?

3. What surprises you most about Jesus?

What prayer would help you just now?

Chapter 5: Passover to Pentecost

1. What shocks you most about the crucifixion?

2. What helps or challenges you about Jesus' death and resurrection?

3. What interests you most about the Holy Spirit?

What prayer support would you like now?

APPENDIX 1

Chronology with Jerusalem Festivals

Birth and Boyhood of Jesus

Description	Location	Scripture
The divinity of Christ	.	Jn 1:1-5
Birth of John the Baptist announced	Jerusalem	Lk 1:5-25
Betrothal of the Virgin Mary	Nazareth	Mt 1:18 Lk 1:27
The annunciation of the birth of Jesus	Nazareth	Lk 1:26-38
about 120 miles (190 km) – about two weeks travel		
The visitation of Mary to Elizabeth	Judah	Lk 1:39-55
about 120 miles – about two weeks travel		
Her return to Nazareth	Nazareth	Lk 1:56
Joseph's vision	Nazareth	Mt 1:20-25
Birth and infancy of John the Baptist	Judah	Lk 1:57-80
about 90 miles – about ten days travel from Nazareth, and 5 miles (8 km) south of Jerusalem		

Birth of Jesus	Bethlehem	Lk 2:1-7
Adoration by the shepherds	Bethlehem	Lk 2:8-16
Circumcision	Bethlehem	Mt 1:25 Lk 2:21
about 5 miles – about half a day's travel		
Presentation and purification	Jerusalem	Lk 2:22-29
The Genealogies	.	Mt 1:1-17 Lk 3:23-38
about 5 miles – about half a day's travel		
Adoration by the wise men	Bethlehem	Mt 2:1-12
Flight into Egypt	Egypt	Mt 2:13-15
Massacre of the innocents	Bethlehem	Mt 2:16-18
about 100 miles (160 km) – about ten days' travel		
Return to Nazareth	Nazareth	Mt 2:19-23 Lk 2:39
Childhood of Jesus	Nazareth	Lk 2:40
about 90 miles (145 km) – about ten days' travel		
With the teachers in the Temple	Jerusalem	Lk 2:41-50
about 90 miles – about ten days' travel		
Youth of Jesus	Nazareth	Lk 2:51-52

From John the Baptist to the First Passover

Description	Location	Scripture
Ministry of John the Baptist	Bethabara	Mt 3:1-4 Mt 1:1-8 Lk 3:1-6 Jn 1:6-15
Baptisms by John	Bethabara	Mt 3:5 Mk 1:5 Lk 3:7
First testimony of the Baptist to Christ	Bethabara	Mt 3:11,12 Mk 1:7,8 Lk 3:15-18
Baptism of Jesus by John	Bethabara	Mt 3:13-17 Mk 1:9-11 Lk 3:21,22
Temptation of Jesus in Wilderness Of Judea	Judea	Mt 4:1-11 Mk 1:12,13 Lk 4:1-13
John the Baptist's second testimony	Bethabara	Jn 1:19-35
Call of the first disciples	Bethabara	Jn 1:35-51
First Miracle at Cana	Cana	Jn 2:1-11
Visit to Capernaum	Capernaum	Jn 2:12
First Passover: Cleansing the Temple	Jerusalem	Jn 2:13-23
Discourse with Nicodemus	Jerusalem	Jn 3:1-21

Israel from space
Lake Galilee, Jordan Valley to Dead Sea
Jerusalem east of north end of Dead Sea

From the First Passover to the Second Passover

Description	Location	Scripture
The Baptist's last testimony	Aenon	Jn 3:22-36
Jesus visits Samaria	Sychar	Jn 4:1-42
Return to Cana	Cana	Jn 4:43-46
Nobleman's son healed	Cana	Jn 4:46-54
Brief visit to Jerusalem	Jerusalem	Jn 5:1-47
Miracle at pool of Bethesda	Jerusalem	Jn 5:1-47
John the Baptist in prison	Machaerus	Mt 4:12,17 Mk 1:14,15
Jesus preaches in Galilee	Galilee	Lk 4:14,15
Jesus preaches at Nazareth	Nazareth	Mk 6:1 Lk 4:15-30
Jesus preaches at Capernaum	Capernaum	Mt 4:13-16 Lk 4:31
Call of Andrew, Peter, James and John	Capernaum	Mt 4:18-22 Mk 1:16-20 Lk 5:1-11
Miracle draught of fishes	Capernaum	Lk 5:1-11
Demoniac healed	Capernaum	Mk 1:23-27 Lk 4:33-36
Peter's mother-in-law healed	Capernaum	Mt 8:14,15 Mk 1:29-31 Lk 4:38,39
Many sick and diseased healed	Capernaum	Mt 8:16,17 Mk 1:32-34 Lk 4:40,41

Retirement for solitary prayer	Galilee	Mk 1:35 Lk 4:42
Circuit through Galilee	Galilee	Mk 1:35-39 Lk 4:42-44
Miraculous Healing of a leper	Galilee	Mt 8:1-4 Mk 1:40-45 Lk 5:12-16
Retirement for a solitary prayer	Galilee	Mk 1:45 Lk 5:16
Miraculous Healing of a paralytic	Capernaum	Mt 9:1-8 Mk 2:1-12 Lk 5:18-26
Call of Matthew (Levi) Discourse at the feast	Capernaum	Mt 9:9-17 Mk 2:13-22 Lk 5:27-39
Disciples pluck the ears of corn	Galilee	Mt 12:1-8 Mk 2:23-28 Lk 6:1-5
The man with a withered hand healed	Capernaum	Mt 12:9-14 Mk 3:1-6 Lk 6:6-11
Retirement for solitary prayer	Galilee	Lk 6:12
Call of the Twelve Apostles	Hill of Hattin?	Mt 10:2-4 Mk 3:13-19 Lk 6:13-16
Sermon on the Mount	Hill of Hattin?	Mt 5-7 Lk 6:17-49
Parable of House on rock or sand	Hill of Hattin?	Mt 7:24-29 Lk 6:47-49
Centurion's servant healed	Hill of Hattin?	Mt 8:5-13 Lk 7:1-10

Widow of Nain's son raised	Nain	Lk 7:11-17
Message from John the Baptist	Capernaum	Mt 11:2-19 Lk 7:18-35
Jesus tells of John the Baptist	Capernaum	Mt 11:2-19 Lk 7:18-35
The sinful woman	Capernaum?	Lk 7:36-50
Parable of two debtors	Capernaum?	Lk 7:41,42
Galilee tour with the twelve	Galilee	Lk 8:1-3
Demoniac healed	Capernaum	Mt 12:22
Blasphemy against Holy Spirit	Capernaum	Mt 12:24-37 Mk 3:22-30
The unclean spirit	Capernaum	Mt 12:43-46
Jesus' relatives	Capernaum	Mt 12:46 Mk 3:31
Parables: The Sower	Galilee	Mt 13:1-9,18-23 Mk 4:1,14-20 Lk 8:4,11-15
Parables: The Tares	Galilee	Mt 13:24
Parables: The Mustard seed	Galilee	Mt 13:31 Mk 4:30
Parables: The Leaven	Galilee	Mt 13:33 Lk 13:20,21
Parables: The Candle	Galilee	Mt 5:15 Mk 4:21 Lk 8:16
Parables: The Candle	Galilee	Mt 5:15 Mk 4:21 Lk 11:33
Parables: The Treasure	Galilee	Mt 13:44
Parables: The Pearl	Galilee	Mt 13:45

Parables: The Drawnet	Galilee	Mt 13:47
Parables: Seed grows secretly	Galilee	Mk 4:26-29
Jesus calms the storm	Lake Galilee	Mt 8:24-27 Mk 4:37-41 Lk 8:23-25
Gergesene demoniacs set free	Gergesa	Mt 8:28-34 Mk 5:1-15 Lk 8:27-35
Parables: The Bridegroom	Capernaum	Mt 9:15
Parable: Cloth on old garment	Capernaum	Mt 9:16 Mk 2:21 Lk 5:36
Parable: new wine in old skins	Capernaum	Mt 9:17 Mk 2:22 Lk 5:37,38
Woman with issue of blood	Gennesaret	Mt 9:18 Mk 5:22 Lk 8:41
Jairus' daughter raised	Capernaum	Mt 9:18 Mk 5:22 Lk 8:41
Two blind men healed	Capernaum	Mt 9:27,30
Dumb spirit cast out	Capernaum	Mt 9:32,33
Mission of Twelve Apostles	Capernaum	Mt 10:1 Mk 6:7-12 Lk 9:1-6
Death of John the Baptist	Machaerus	Mt 14:1-12 Mk 6:14-29 Lk 9:7
Feeding of the five thousand **Second Passover crowds gathering**	Bethsaida	Mt 14:13-21 Mk 6:30-44 Lk 9:12-17 Jn 6:1-13

| Jesus walks on the water | Lake Galilee | Mt 14:25 Mk 6:48 Jn 6:19 |
| Bread of Life discourse | Capernaum | Mt 14:34 Jn 6:26-70 |

From the Second Passover to the Third Passover

Description	Location	Scripture
Opposition of Scribes and Pharisees	Capernaum	Mt 15:1
Discourse on Pollution	Capernaum	Mt 15:2-20 Mk 7:1-23
Healing the daughter of the Syrophoenician woman	Phoenicia	Mt 15:21-29 Mk 7:24-30
Deaf and dumb man healed	Tyre, Sidon	Mk 7:32
Healing of many sick people	Decapolis	Mt 15:30,31
Feeding of the four thousand	Gennesaret	Mt 15:32-39 Mk 8:1-9
Parable of the leaven of Pharisees	Gennesaret	Mt 16:1-12 Mk 8:14-22
Healing of the Blind man	Bethsaida	Mk 8:23-27
Peter's confession of Christ	Caesarea Philippi	Mt 16:13-21 Mk 8:27-30
First prediction of the Passion	Caesarea Philippi	Mt 16:21-28 Mk 8:31-38 Lk 9:22-27

The transfiguration	Mt. Hermon	Mt 17:1-8 Mk 9:2-8 Lk 9:28-36
Healing the demoniac child	Mt. Hermon	Mt 17:14-21 Mk 9:14-27 Lk 9:37-42
Second prediction of the Passion	Galilee	Mt 17:22,23 Mk 9:31 Lk 9:43,44
The coin in the fish's mouth	Capernaum	Mt 17:27
Lesson on docility	Capernaum	Mt 18:1-14 Mk 9:33-37 Lk 9:46-48
Lesson on forgiveness	Capernaum	Mt 18:15 Mk 9:43
Lesson on self-denial	Capernaum	Mt 18:18
Parable of the unmerciful servant	Capernaum	Mt 18:23-35
Trip to Jerusalem through Samaria	Samaria	Lk 9:51,52
Jealousy of the Samaritans	Samaria	Lk 9:53
Anger of the 'sons of thunder'	Samaria	Lk 9:54-56
The feast of Tabernacles	Jerusalem	Jn 7:2-10
Discourses	Jerusalem	Jn 7:10-46
Officers sent to arrest Christ	Jerusalem	Jn 7:30,46
The adulteress	Jerusalem	Jn 8:3
Discourses	Jerusalem	Jn 8:12
Christ threatened with stoning	Jerusalem	Jn 8:59

Blind man healed and discourses	Jerusalem	Jn 9:1
Christ the Door; the Good Shepherd	Jerusalem	Jn 10:1
Departure from Jerusalem.		
Mission of the seventy	Judea	Lk 10:1-16
Return of the seventy	Judea	Lk 10:17-24
Parable of the Good Samaritan	Judea	Lk 10:30-37
Visit to Martha, Mary	Bethany	Lk 10:38-42
Jesus teaches his disciples to pray	Judea	Lk 11:1-13
Parable of importunate friend	Judea	Lk 11:5-8
Mute demoniac healed	Judea	Mt 12:22-45 Lk 11:14
Pharisees' blasphemy rebuked	Judea	Mt 12:22-45 Lk 11:14
Discourses: repentant Ninevites	Judea	Mt 12:41 Lk 11:29-36
Providence to birds and flowers	Judea	Lk 12:1-12
Parable of the rich fool	Judea	Lk 12:13-21
Parable of servants watching	Judea	Lk 12:35-40
Parable of the wise steward	Judea	Lk 12:42-48
The murdered Galileans	Judea	Lk 13:1-5
The barren fig tree	Judea	Lk 13:6-9

Healing of woman with an infirmity	Judea	Lk 13:10-17
Feast of Dedication in Jerusalem	Jerusalem	Jn 10:22-30
Attempt to stone Jesus	Jerusalem	Jn 10:31
Jesus retires across Jordan	Peraea	Jn 10:40
Are there few that be saved?	Peraea	Lk 13:23-30
The message to Herod	Paraea	Lk 13:31-33
Healing of the man with dropsy	Peraea	Lk 14:1-6
Parable of the great supper	Peraea	Lk 14:15-24
Parable of tower, warring king	Paraea	Lk 14:28-33
Parable of the lost sheep	Peraea	Mt 18:12,13 Lk 15:1-7
Parable of the lost coin	Peraea	Lk 15:8-10
Parable of the prodigal son	Peraea	Lk 15:11-32
Parable of the unjust steward	Peraea	Lk 16:1-13
Parable of the rich man and Lazarus	Peraea	Lk 16:19-31
Parable of the unprofitable servants	Peraea	Lk 17:7-10
Sickness of Lazarus	Bethany	Jn 11:1-10
Jesus goes from Peraea to Bethany	Peraea	Jn 11:11-16

Miraculous resurrection of Lazarus	Bethany	Jn 11:17-46
The council: Advice of Caiaphas	Jerusalem	Jn 11:47-53
Jesus retires to the town of Ephraim	Ephraim	Jn 11:54
Last journey to Jerusalem	Samaria border	Mt 19:1 Mk 10:1 Lk 17:11
Healing of the ten lepers	Samaria border	Lk 17:12-19
Parable of the unjust judge	Samaria border	Lk 18:1-8
Parable: Pharisee and the publican	Samaria border	Lk 18:9-14
The question of divorce	Samaria border	Mt 19:3-12 Mk 10:2-12
Jesus blesses little children	Samaria border	Mt 19:13-15 Mk 10:13-16 Lk 18:15-17
The rich young ruler	Samaria border	Mt 19:16-22 Mk 10:17-22 Lk 18:18-23
Parable: Labourers in the vineyard	Samaria border	Mt 20:1-16
Third prediction of the Passion	Samaria border	Mt 20:17-19 Mk 10:32-34 Lk 18:31-34

Request of James and John	Samaria border	Mt 20:20-28 Mk 10:35-45
Healing of Blind Bartimaeus	Near Jericho	Mt 20:29-34 Mk 10:46-52 Lk 18:35-43
Jesus at the house of Zacchaeus	Jericho	Lk 19:1-10
Parable of the pounds	Jericho	Lk 19:11-28

Old City of Jerusalem today, Temple Mount central Old Zion City south in the foreground down the ridge Kidron Valley and Mount of Olives east at right Calvary outside Old City north-west at left

Holy Week: Confrontation

Description	Location	Scripture
The supper in Simon's house	Bethany	Mt 26:6-13 Mk 14:3-9 Jn 12:1-9
Mary anoints Jesus	Bethany	Mt 26:7-13 Mk 14:3-8 Jn 12:3-8
Triumphal entry into the city	Jerusalem	Mt 21:1-11 Mk 11:1-10 Lk 19:29-44 Jn 12:12-19
Survey of the Temple	Jerusalem	Mr 11:11
Retirement to Bethany	Bethany	Mr 11:11
Withering of the barren fig-tree	Olivet	Mt 21:18-19 Mk 11:12-14
Second cleansing of the Temple	Jerusalem	Mt 21:12-17 Mk 11:15-19 Lk 19:45-48
Retirement to Bethany	Bethany	Mt 21:17 Mk 11:19
The lesson of the fig-tree	Olivet	Mt 21:20-22 Mk 11:20-25
Discourses in the Temple:	Jerusalem	Mk 11:26
The rulers' question	Jerusalem	Mt 21:23-27 Mk 11:27-33 Lk 20:1-8
The parable of the two sons	Jerusalem	Mt 21:28-32

Parable of the wicked husbandmen	Jerusalem	Mt 21:33-46 Mk 12:1-12 Lk 20:9-19
Parable of the wedding garment	Jerusalem	Mt 22:1-14
The subtle questions:-		
1) of the Pharisees – the tribute money	Jerusalem	Mt 22:15-22 Mk 12:13-17 Lk 20:20-26
2) of the Sadducees – the resurrection	Jerusalem	Mt 22:23-33 Mk 12:18-27 Lk 20:27-39
3) of the Lawyer – the great commandment	Jerusalem	Mt 22:34-40 Mk 12:28-34
Our Lord's counter question	Jerusalem	Mt 22:41-46 Mk 12:35-37 Lk 20:41-44
Scribes and Pharisees denounced	Jerusalem	Mt 23:13-33
The widow's mite	Jerusalem	Mk 12:41-44 Lk 21:1-4
The coming of the Greeks	Jerusalem	Jn 12:20-36
The departure to the Mt of Olives	Olivet	Mt 24:1-3 Mr 13:1-3
Prediction 1: the destruction of Jerusalem	Olivet	Mt 24:3-28 Mk 13:3-23 Lk 21:5-24
Parable of fig-tree and all the trees	Olivet	Mt 24:32,33 Mk 13:28,29

		Lk 21:29-32
Prediction 2: of the second coming	Olivet	Mt 24:28-51 Mk 13:23-37 Lk 21:24-36
Parable of the householder	Olivet	Mk 13:34
Parables:- The ten virgins	Olivet	Mt 25:1-13
Parables:- The talents	Olivet	Mt 25:14-30
Parables:- The sheep and the goats	Olivet	Mt 25:31-46
The Sanhedrin in council	Jerusalem	Mt 26:3-5 Mk 14:1-2 Lk 22:1-2
Compact of the traitor	Jerusalem	Mt 26:14-16 Mk 14:10,11 Lk 22:3-6

The Last Supper

Preparation of the Passover	Jerusalem	Mt 26:17-19 Mk 14:12-16 Lk 22:7-13
Washing the apostles' feet	Jerusalem	Jn 13:1-17
The breaking of bread	Jerusalem	Mt 26:26 Mk 14:22 Lk 22:19
'One of you shall betray me'	Jerusalem	Mt 26:21 Mk 14:18 Lk 22:21 Jn 13:21
'Is it I ?'	Jerusalem	Mt 26:22-25 Mk 14:19
Giving of the bread	Jerusalem	Jn 13:26,27
Departure of Judas Iscariot	Jerusalem	Jn 13:30
Peter warned	Jerusalem	Mt 26:34 Mk 14:30 Lk 22:34 Jn 13:38
Blessing the cup	Jerusalem	Mt 26:27,28 Mk 14:23,24 Lk 22:17
The discourses after supper	Jerusalem	Jn 14:1-16:33
Christ's prayer for his apostles	Jerusalem	Jn 17:1-17:26
The hymn	Jerusalem	Mt 26:30 Mk 14:26

Western Wall of the Temple Mount and Plaza
Mount of Olives east in the background

Gethsemane and Trials

The agony	Gethsemane	Mt 26:37 Mk 14:33 Lk 22:39 Jn 18:1
The thrice-repeated prayer	Gethsemane	Mt 26:39-44 Mk 14:36-39 Lk 22:42
Sweat and angel support	Gethsemane	Lk 22:43,44
The sleep of the apostles	Gethsemane	Mt 26:40-45 Mk 14:37-41 Lk 22:45,46
Betrayal by Judas	Gethsemane	Mt 26:47-50 Mk 14:34,44 Lk 22:47 Jn 18:2-5
Peter smites Malchus	Gethsemane	Mt 26:51 Mk 14:47 Lk 22:50 Jn 18:10
Jesus heals the ear of Malchus	Gethsemane	Lk 22:51
Jesus forsaken by disciples	Gethsemane	Mt 26:56 Mk 14:50
Jesus led to Annas	Jerusalem	Jn 18:12,13
Jesus tried by Caiaphas	Jerusalem	Mt 26:57 Mk 14:53 Lk 22:54 Jn 18:15
Peter follows Jesus	Jerusalem	Mt 26:58 Mk 14:54 Lk 22:55 Jn 18:15
The high priest's adjuration	Jerusalem	Mt 26:63 Mk 14:61
Jesus condemned, buffeted, mocked	Jerusalem	Mt 26:66,67 Mk 14:64,65 Lk 22:63-65
Peter's denial of Christ	Jerusalem	Mt 26:69-75 Mk 14:66-72

		Lk 22:54-62 Jn 18:17-27
Jesus before Pilate	Jerusalem	Mt 27:1,2 Mk 15:1 Lk 23:1 Jn 18:28
Repentance of Judas	Jerusalem	Mt 27:3
Pilate comes out to the people	Jerusalem	Jn 18:29
Pilate speaks to Jesus privately	Jerusalem	Jn 18:33
Pilate orders him to be scourged	Jerusalem	Mt 27:26 Mk 15:15 Jn 19:1
Jesus crowned with thorns	Jerusalem	Mt 27:29 Mk 15:17 Jn 19:2
'Behold the man'	Jerusalem	Jn 19:5
Jesus accused formally	Jerusalem	Mt 27:11 Mk 15:2 Lk 23:2
Jesus sent by Pilate to Herod	Jerusalem	Lk 23:6-11
Jesus mocked, arrayed in purple	Jerusalem	Lk 23:6-11
'Behold your King'	Jerusalem	Jn 19:14
Pilate desires to release him	Jerusalem	Mt 27:15 Mk 15:6 Lk 23:17 Jn 19:12
Pilate's wife message	Jerusalem	Mt 27:19
Pilate washes his hands	Jerusalem	Mt 27:24
Pilate releases Barabbas	Jerusalem	Mt 27:26

Crucifixion

Pilate delivers Jesus to be crucified	Jerusalem	Mt 27:26 Mk 15:15 Lk 23:25 Jn 19:16
Simon of Cyrene carries the cross	Jerusalem	Mt 27:32 Mk 15:21 Lk 23:26
They give Jesus vinegar and gall	Golgotha	Mt 27:34 Mk 15:23 Lk 23:36
They nail him to the cross	Golgotha	Mt 27:35 Mk 15:24,25 Lk 23:33 Jn 19:18
The superscription	Golgotha	Mt 27:37 Mk 15:26 Lk 23:38 Jn 19:19
1) Father, forgive them	Golgotha	Lk 23:34
His garments parted, and vesture allotted	Golgotha	Mt 27:35 Mk 15:24 Lk 23:34 Jn 19:23
Passers-by rail, the two thieves revile	Golgotha	Mt 27:39-44 Mk 15:29-32 Lk 23:35
The penitent thief	Golgotha	Lk 23:40
2) Today you will be with me ...	Golgotha	Lk 23:43
3) Woman, behold your son. ...	Golgotha	Jn 19:26,27

Darkness over all the land	Golgotha	Mt 27:45 Mk 15:33 Lk 23:44,45
4) My God, my God, why ... ?	Golgotha	Mt 27:46 Mk 15:34
5) I thirst	Golgotha	Jn 19:28
The vinegar	Golgotha	Mt 27:48 Mk 15:36 Jn 19:29
6) It is finished	Golgotha	Jn 19:30
7) Father, into your hands ...	Golgotha	Lk 23:46
Rending of the veil	Jerusalem	Mt 27:51 Mk 15:38 Lk 23:45
Graves opened, saints resurrected	Jerusalem	Mt 27:52
Testimony of centurion	Golgotha	Mt 27:54 Mk 15:39 Lk 23:47
Watching of the women	Golgotha	Mt 27:55 Mk 15:40 Lk 23:49
The piercing of his side	Golgotha	Jn 19:34
Taking down from the cross	The Garden	Mt 27:57-60 Mk 15:46 Lk 23:53 Jn 19:38-42
Burial by Joseph of Arimathea, Nicodemus	The Garden	Mt 27:57-60 Mk 15:46 Lk 23:53 Jn 19:38-42
A guard placed over the sealed stone	Garden	Mt 27:65-66

Resurrection

Description	Location	Scripture
Women carry spices to the tomb	The Garden	Mt 28:1 Mk 16:1,2 Lk 24:1
The angel had rolled away the stone	Garden	Mt 28:2
Women announce the resurrection	Jerusalem	Mt 28:8 Lk 24:9,10 Jn 20:1,2
Peter and John run to the tomb	Garden	Lk 24:12 Jn 20:3
The women return to the tomb	Garden	Lk 24:1
The guards report to the chief priests	Jerusalem	Mt 28:11-15
RESURRECTION APPEARANCES		
1) To Mary Magdalene	Garden	Mk 16:9,10 Jn 20:14-18
2) To the women returning home	Garden	Mt 28:9-10
3) To two disciples going to Emmaus	Emmaus Road	Mk 16:12 Lk 24:13
4) To Peter	Jerusalem	1Co 15:5 Lk 24:34
5) To 10 disciples in the upper room	Jerusalem	Lk 24:33 Jn 20:19-23

6) To 11 disciples in the upper room	Jerusalem	Mk 16:14 Jn 20:26-29
7) To 500 at once	Unknown	1 Cor 15:6
8) To James	Unknown	1 Cor 15:6
9) To 7 disciples at the lake shore	Galilee	Jn 21:1-11
10) To 11 disciples on a mountain	Galilee	Mt 28:18-20
11) To disciples eating together	Jerusalem	Acts 1:4-5
12) THE ASCENSION	Mt of Olives Bethany	Mk 16:19 Lk 24:50-51 Acts 1:6-9

This chronology and charts are adapted and used with permission from Believe:
http://mb-soft.com/believe/txh/gospgosp.htm

Ancient tomb

APPENDIX 2

The Feast Days

Leviticus 23 briefly covers all of the feasts of the Lord. There are three annual feasts that the Lord commanded all of Israel to celebrate in Jerusalem — Passover, Pentecost, and Tabernacles. Here is Leviticus 23 from the Easy-to-Read Version (biblegateway.com).

The Special Festivals

The LORD said to Moses, ² "Tell the Israelites: You will announce the LORD's chosen festivals as holy meetings. These are my special festivals.

Sabbath

³ "Work for six days, but the seventh day, the Sabbath will be a special day of rest, a holy meeting. You must not do any work. It is a day of rest to honour the LORD in all your homes.

Festival of Passover (Exodus 12:1-11; Numbers 28:16-25)

⁴ "These are the LORD's chosen festivals. You will announce the holy meetings at the times chosen for them. ⁵ The LORD's Passover is on the 14th day of the first month just before dark.

Festival of Unleavened Bread

6 "The LORD's Festival of Unleavened Bread is on the 15th day of the same month. You will eat unleavened bread for seven days. 7 On the first day of this festival, you will have a special meeting. You must not do any work on that day. 8 For seven days, you will bring sacrifices offered as gifts to the LORD. Then there will be another special meeting on the seventh day. You must not do any work on that day."

Festival of the First Harvests (First Fruits)

9 The LORD said to Moses, 10 "Tell the Israelites: You will enter the land that I will give you and reap its harvest. At that time you must bring in the first sheaf of your harvest to the priest. 11 The priest will lift the sheaf to show it was offered before the LORD. Then you will be accepted. The priest will present the sheaf on Sunday morning.

12 "On the day when you present the sheaf, you will offer a one-year-old male lamb. There must be nothing wrong with that lamb. That lamb will be a burnt offering to the LORD. 13 You must also offer a grain offering of 16 cups of fine flour mixed with olive oil. You must also offer 1 quart of wine. The smell of that offering will please the LORD. 14 You must not eat any of the new grain, or fruit, or bread made from the new grain until you bring that offering to your God. This law will always continue through your generations, wherever you live.

Festival of Harvest or Weeks (Pentecost, Numbers 28:26-31)

15 "From that Sunday morning (the day you bring the sheaf to be presented to God), count seven weeks. 16 On the Sunday following the seventh week (that is, 50 days later),

you will bring a new grain offering to the LORD. **17** On that day bring two loaves of bread from your homes. That bread will be lifted up to show it was offered to God. Use yeast and 16 cups of flour to make those loaves of bread. That will be your gift to the LORD from your first harvest.

18 "With these grain offerings bring one bull, one ram, and seven one-year-old male lambs for burnt offerings to the LORD. There must be nothing wrong with these animals. Offer them together with the grain offerings and the drink offerings. The smell of these offerings made by fire will be pleasing to the LORD. **19** You will also offer one male goat for a sin offering and two one-year-old male lambs as a fellowship offering.

20 "The priest will lift them up with the bread from the first harvest to show they were offered with the two lambs before the LORD. They are holy to the LORD. They will belong to the priest. **21** On that same day you will call a holy meeting. You must not do any work. This law continues forever in all your homes.

22 "Also, when you harvest the crops on your land, don't cut all the way to the corners of your field. Don't pick up the grain that falls on the ground. Leave it for poor people and for foreigners traveling through your country. I am the LORD your God."

Festival of Trumpets (Numbers 29:1-6)

23 Again the LORD said to Moses, **24** "Tell the Israelites: On the first day of the seventh month, you must have a special day of rest. Blow the trumpet to remind the people that this is a holy meeting. **25** You must not do any work. You must bring an offering as a gift to the LORD."

Day of Atonement (Leviticus 16:1-34; Numbers 29:7-11)

26 The Lord said to Moses, **27** "The Day of Atonement will be on the tenth day of the seventh month. There will be a holy meeting. You must not eat food, and you must bring an offering as a gift to the Lord. **28** You must not do any work on that day, because it is the Day of Atonement. On that day the priests will go before the Lord and perform the ceremony that makes you pure.

29 "Anyone who refuses to fast on this day must be separated from their people. **30** If anyone does any work on this day, I will destroy that person from among the people. **31** You must not do any work at all. This is a law that continues forever for you, wherever you live. **32** It will be a special day of rest for you. You must not eat food. You will start this special day of rest on the evening following the ninth day of the month. This special day of rest continues from that evening until the next evening."

Festival of Tabernacles (Booths, Numbers 29:12-40)

33 Again the Lord said to Moses, **34** "Tell the Israelites: On the 15th day of the seventh month is the Festival of Shelters. This festival to the Lord will continue for seven days. **35** There will be a holy meeting on the first day. You must not do any work. **36** You will bring offerings as gifts to the Lord for seven days. On the eighth day, you will have another holy meeting. You must not do any work. You will bring an offering as a gift to the Lord.

37 "These are the Lord's special festivals. There will be holy meetings during these festivals. You will bring offerings as gifts to the Lord—burnt offerings, grain offerings, sacrifices, and drink offerings. You will bring these gifts at the right time. **38** You will celebrate these festivals in addition to remembering the LORD's Sabbath days. You will offer these gifts in addition to your other gifts and any offerings you give as payment for your special promises. They will be in addition to any special offerings you want to give to the LORD.

39 "On the 15th day of the seventh month, when you have gathered in the crops of the land, you will celebrate the LORD's festival for seven days. The first day will be a special day of rest, and then the eighth day will also be a special day of rest. **40** On the first day you will take good fruit from fruit trees. And you will take branches from palm trees, poplar trees, and willow trees by the brook. You will celebrate before the LORD your God for seven days. **41** You will celebrate this festival to with the LORD for seven days each year. This law will continue forever. You will celebrate this festival in the seventh month. **42** You will live in temporary shelters for seven days. All the people born in Israel will live in them. **43** Why? So all your descendants will know that I made the Israelites live in temporary shelters during the time I brought them out of Egypt. I am the LORD your God."

44 So Moses told the Israelites about all the special meetings to honour the LORD.

An Overview

God gave Moses the dates and details of the annual festivals.

1. Passover *(Pesach) - Nisan 14-15*
2. Unleavened Bread *(Chag Hamotzi) - Nisan 15-22*
3. First Fruits *(Yom Habikkurim) - Nisan 16-17*
4. Pentecost *(Shavuot) - Sivan 6-7*
5. Trumpets *(Yom Teruah) - Tishri 1*

6. Atonement *(Yom Kippur) - Tishri 10*
7. Tabernacles *(Sukkot) - Tishri 15-22*

Each month began with a new moon. Passover fell on the first full moon of spring. The first three feasts, Passover, Unleavened Bread, and First Fruits in March/April included the spring harvests of wheat and barley. The fourth one, Pentecost, marked the start of the summer harvest in late May or early June. The last three feasts, Trumpets, Atonement, and Tabernacles in September/October included the autumn/fall harvests of grapes, figs, and olives.

The Spring Festivals

(1) Passover. The festival year began with Passover on the 14th day of the first month (Nisan 14) when the unblemished lamb was slain. The angel of death "passed over" the Jewish homes with the blood of the lamb on their doorposts. Our Lord was sacrificed on Passover, the Day of Preparation.

(2) Unleavened Bread. This feast began on the next day (Nisan 15) and lasted for seven days. Today the unleavened bread (Matzah) is striped and pierced, as was Jesus' body.

(3) First Fruits. Celebrated on the day after the Sabbath, they brought the early crops of wheat and barley to wave the sheaf before the Lord. They sacrificed Passover lambs on the 14th of Nisan; then the first day of Unleavened Bread was the 15th; with the Feast of First Fruits celebrated on the third day on the 16th of Nisan. This third-day celebration points to Jesus' resurrection.

(4) Pentecost. On the Sunday after the seventh Sabbath (50 days after Passover) they offered two loaves of bread with leaven/yeast and new meat offerings, marking the beginning of the summer harvest. The Holy Spirit was first poured out at this festival in Jerusalem.

The Autumn/Fall Festivals

(5) Trumpets. The 1st day of the seventh month was celebrated with blowing the ram's horn. The trumpet was the signal for the field workers to come into the Temple. It reminds some people of the ram caught in the thorn bush that became a substitute sacrifice for Isaac, Abraham's son, on Mount Moriah.

(6) Atonement. This highest of holy days fell on the 10th day of the seventh month. A day of fasting and sacrifices, it was the only time once a year when the High Priest sprinkled blood on the golden mercy seat of the Ark of the Covenant in the Holy of Holies behind the thick curtain in the tabernacle and then later in the temple. Our atonement is found in Jesus' blood that was shed for us.

(7) Tabernacles. The 15th day of the seventh month commenced a week of celebrating in booths, a reminder of God's care during the 40 years of Israel's wandering in the wilderness. He led them there with a pillar of fire and smoke above the tabernacle. He leads us by his Spirit.

A Winter Festival: The Feast of Dedication (Hanukah) in December celebrated the cleansing of the temple in 165 BC when olive oil burned for eight days during the Maccabean revolt against the Greek empire. Jesus attended this optional feast before his final Passover sacrifice the following April.

APPENDIX 3

The Gospels

The Gospels are not biography although much of their good news is biographical. They tell the story of God's love revealed perfectly in Jesus.

Matthew tells the love story

A despised, hated tax collector for Rome, Matthew admired Jesus and left his lucrative business to travel on foot with Jesus and the growing crowd of his followers. A staunch Jew, Matthew likely wrote his love story in Aramaic, the lingua franca of the Middle East at that time.

They copied their Scriptures (our Old Testament) in Hebrew scrolls, but from the time of the Jews' return from captivity in Babylon, around 538 BC, they spoke Aramaic, a Semitic language similar to Hebrew, which spread through the Middle East. It became the native language of Palestine used by Jesus and his followers.[67] Matthew quotes liberally from the Hebrew Scriptures, showing that Jesus fulfilled their prophecies. Matthew's story was reproduced in common Greek and used widely at that time following Alexander the Great's conquests.

Matthew the evangelist wrote especially for Jews. He begins his gospel by presenting Jesus Christ as the son of David, the son of Abraham. He ends his gospel with the Great Commission

---

[67] Matthew 1:21, The Passion Translation.

declaring that Jesus sends his followers into all nations. In Jesus, God's covenant embraces the whole world.

This radical evangelistic missionary gospel shocked traditional Jews. Matthew insists that Jesus was the long-awaited Messiah, backing up his claims with many quotations from the Old Testament. He argues that Jesus did not do away with the Scriptures, but fulfilled them.[68] He emphasizes the missionary nature of Jesus' ministry and of his church.

This gospel continually confronted the Jewish Christian community as well as other Jews. Here is a persistent and urgent call to mission. The good news is for all people, not only for Jews. Matthew begins his Gospel by telling of the coming of Jesus the Messiah who proclaims God's universal kingdom. The figure of Jesus the Messiah is announced by John the Baptist, as prophesied.

The beginning of the ministry in Galilee shows Christ's design for life in God's kingdom, again fulfilling prophecy. Chapters 5-7 gather the words of Jesus together in The Sermon on the Mount in which we are challenged to seek first the kingdom of God. Here is the kingdom charter, the ethics of kingdom living. The chapters that follow demonstrate God's kingdom in the works of Jesus.

Matthew gathers the discourses of Jesus as teaching segments throughout his narrative. He often uses the phrase "kingdom of heaven" for the kingdom of God in typical Jewish reverence for the word *God*.

Jesus' ministry is summarized in Matthew 4:23 as teaching in their synagogues, preaching the good news of the kingdom, and

---

[68] Matthew 5:17.

healing every disease and sickness. This statement introduces the words and works of Jesus in chapters 5-9. Then in Matthew 9:35, the same statement is repeated. Here it introduces the mission of Jesus' followers.

The mission discourse, commencing from Matthew 9:35, tells of Jesus' plan for the spread of God's kingdom. His disciples will continue his ministry. They will proclaim the kingdom of God.

The chapters following the mission discourse show the radical nature of the mystery of God's kingdom. This mystery is revealed by Jesus to those committed to him, but concealed from others, as indicated in the parable discourses of chapter 13.

Matthew, the only gospel writer to use the word 'church', points out that Jesus' church has his authority.[69] The church is the agent of God's kingdom and manifests the kingdom in the world.

Tensions with the keepers of Israel's traditions reached a flash point and boiled over into Jesus' arrest and execution. That is the volatile setting in which Jesus pressed his authority and invitation as his ministry ended. The king is crowned with thorns and crucified. Apparent defeat in death is then turned into the amazing victory of resurrection. Christ the King reigns. We all ultimately acknowledge his reign in the end. In Jesus' victory, we see God's kingdom fulfilled.

---

[69] Matthew 16:18-19; 18:17-18.

Mark tells the love story

Probably as a young man in Jerusalem, Mark knew and hung around Jesus and his followers. His love story is a condensed version, the shortest account, and possibly the first cab off the rank. It's likely that Matthew and Luke both used much of Mark's story in their similar stories, now called the three Synoptic Gospels.

Mark may have been the young man he alone refers to who ran off leaving his linen sheet with the mob who grabbed him in Gethsemane when Jesus was arrested late at night. His family may have lived in a big house where many met to pray and it may have had the large upper room where Jesus ate the Passover. Mark, possibly known as John Mark, joined Paul and Mark's cousin Barnabas and then joined Barnabas again on missionary journeys, and was with Paul in Rome. He traveled with Peter who called him 'my son' and most likely gave him most of the information he used in his Gospel. Jerome, a leader in the early church, told how Mark established the church in Alexandria in Egypt. [70]

Mark gives a vigorous, concise account of Jesus. The narrative moves swiftly. A brief prologue leads immediately into Jesus' ministry as he appears proclaiming and demonstrating the kingdom of God. Kingdom life fills the pages.

Central to that drama is the cross. Mark has been described as a Passion narrative with an introduction. Jesus is introduced as the Son of God in the first verse. Chapters 1-8 reveal the mystery

---

[70] Mark 14:12-16, 50-52; Acts 1:12-14; 12:12, 25; 13:5, 13; 15:36-39; Colossians 4:10; 2 Timothy 4:11;

1 Peter 5:13; and http://www.ldolphin.org/johnmark.html.

of the Son of God seen in Jesus' three-year ministry, based in Galilee.

Then the drama shifts in chapter 8, with Peter's confession that Jesus is the Christ, the Messiah. Jesus immediately predicts his death and prepares his disciples for it. The Messiah must sacrifice his life. The way of the Son of Man is the way of the cross. Chapters 11-16 describe that final week in Jerusalem.

Holy Week, the last week of the earthly life of Jesus, may be summarized this way as a general guide. The different Gospels record different events, each one telling the Gospel, the good news, in their own way. So this arrangement is just an estimate of the sequence of the momentous developments in Holy Week.

This traditional summary of events in Holy Week follows the outline in Mark's Gospel:

Palm Sunday - Day of Demonstration

> Mark 11:1-11 (Zech 9:9) - Jesus enters Jerusalem
> Monday - Day of Authority
> Mark 11:12-19 - fig tree rebuked; temple cleansed
> Tuesday - Day of Conflict
> Mark 11:20 - 13:36 - debates with leaders
> Wednesday - Day of Preparation
> Mark 14:1-11 - anointed at Bethany
> Thursday - Day of Farewell
> Mark 14:12-42 - last supper
> Good Friday - Day of Crucifixion
> Mark 14:43 – 15:47 - trials and death
> Saturday - Day of Sabbath
> Mark 15:46-47 - tomb sealed
> Easter Sunday - Day of Resurrection
> Mark 16:1-18 - resurrection appearances

Note, however, that scholars differ concerning the events of the days of this incredible week. See Appendix 4: Alternative Chronology.

These passages remind us of events from the most momentous week in all history, and indeed in all eternity. The Lamb of God, slain from the foundation of the world, took our sin upon himself, died in our place, and conquered death. He alone is the Saviour of the World. All who believe in him, all who trust him, will not die but live forever with him.

Luke tells the love story

Physician and historian, Luke gives us unique accounts of the earliest days in Jesus' life. The only Gentile author in the Bible, he addressed his two books, Luke-Acts, to his Gentile friend Theophilus. He provides carefully researched historical insights into Jesus and his followers. He alone records Jesus' famous and confronting parables of the Good Samaritan and the Prodigal Son.[71]

Dr. Luke carefully researched the accounts of healing and miracles. He joined the teams on Paul's second and third missionary journeys through Turkey (then called Asia or Asia Minor) and Greece, and on their fateful trip to Rome which included being shipwrecked on Malta. He carefully described those adventures in the 'we passages' in Acts. Paul valued him highly.[72]

Luke wrote with a different emphasis from the other writers of the New Testament who all grew up steeped in Israel's traditions. He writes especially for his community.

Luke the historian describes Jesus' central place in human events. Jesus is the Saviour of the whole world. No one is excluded from God's offer of salvation in Jesus. The poor, despised, and outcasts (such as Gentiles) are especially invited into the kingdom of God. Luke gives a clear, ordered account of the spread of God's kingdom in the ministry of Jesus (Luke's Gospel) and in the early church (The Acts of the Apostles).

---

[71] Luke 1-2; 10:25-37; 15:11-32.

[72] Acts 16:10-17, & 20:5-21:18, & 27:1-28:16; Colossians 4;14; 2 Timothy 4:11; Philemon 24.

Luke the Pilgrim makes "journey" a strong theme in both his books. He tells of events along the way, on the road. This especially applies to Jesus' final journey to Jerusalem. That last journey began after Peter's declaration that Jesus was the Messiah. Jesus explained that it involved his death and resurrection.

Luke the missionary, who often accompanied Paul, tells of the mighty power of the Holy Spirit, first in Jesus, then in his followers, and then in the church's missionary expansion. Luke refers to the Holy Spirit often in both his gospel and The Acts of the Apostles.

Luke the doctor, emphasizes Jesus' compassion and healing power for all who came to him. His gospel abounds with stories of Jesus' care for people. He includes many accounts of Jesus' compassion for the poor and for outcasts.

Luke the evangelist, tells of Jesus' saving power and includes some of the most famous parables which summarise the good news of God's kingdom. Parables of the prodigal son, the lost coin, the good Samaritan, the rich man Lazarus, and the rich fool are unique to Luke's evangelism story. So are the accounts of the Samaritan leper, the sinful woman who anointed Jesus' feet, and Zacchaeus. These were despised people who responded to Jesus.

If you have a Bible with section headings containing cross-references, as in the Good News Bible and New Revised Standard Version, you can easily locate the passages unique to Luke. They have no cross references. Those passages give a feel for Luke's emphasis on telling the good news about the kingdom of God.

John tells the love story

He may have been Jesus' young cousin, a son with his older brother James of the successful fisherman Zebedee who employed others in his business in partnership with Simon and Andrew. John's mother may have been a sister to Jesus' mother Mary, identified by early church leaders as Salome. She wanted Jesus to allow her sons to sit beside him in his new kingdom. She was with John and with Mary at the crucifixion where Jesus committed his mother into John's care. John writes about the disciple whom Jesus loved, usually identified as John himself, who reclined on Jesus' chest at the Last Supper.[73]

John's Gospel and his three letters emphasize God's love revealed in Jesus. Famous verses like John 3:16 and 1 John 3:16 describe that love:

> For God so loved the world that He gave His only begotten Son, that whoever believes in Him should not perish but have everlasting life (John 3:16).

> We know love by this, that he laid down his life for us—and we ought to lay down our lives for one another (1 John 3:16).

John was an eye-witness to the ministry of Jesus. He belonged to the inner circle of disciples with his brother James and with Peter the natural leader. John may have been the youngest of the disciples.

Throughout his Gospel, John emphasized that he recorded what he had seen and heard. He states early in the Gospel that he, with

---

[73] Matthew 20:20-21; 27:56; John 13:23; 19:25.

others, witnessed the life of Jesus the Christ, the Logos, and the living Word of God.

John describes how he was there at the crucifixion witnessing that stupendous, agonizing death. He emphasizes that he wrote so that his readers would believe in Jesus, the Messiah, the Son of God.

> Now Jesus did many other signs in the presence of his disciples, which are not written in this book. But these are written so that you may come to believe that Jesus is the Messiah, the Son of God, and that through believing you may have life in his name. (John 20:30-31)

APPENDIX 4

Alternative Chronology

Some scholars argue for a crucifixion on the Thursday of Holy Week followed by two Sabbath days, the Passover Sabbath on Friday and the regular Sabbath on Saturday.

That chronology correlates with Jesus' predictions:

For just as Jonah was for three days and three nights in the belly of the sea monster, so for three days and three nights the Son of Man will be in the heart of the earth (Matthew 12:40).

Then he took the twelve aside and said to them, 'See, we are going up to Jerusalem, and everything that is written about the Son of Man by the prophets will be accomplished. 32 For he will be handed over to the Gentiles; and he will be mocked and insulted and spat upon. 33 After they have flogged him, they will kill him, and on the third day he will rise again' (Luke 18:31-33).

James Tabor examines the gospel accounts of the Last Supper in his article 'The Last Days of Jesus: A Final "Messianic" Meal', reproduced by the Biblical Archaeology Society (https://www.biblicalarchaeology.org/daily/people-cultures-in-the-bible/jesus-historical-jesus/the-last-days-of-jesus-a-final-messianic-meal/). He writes:

> The confusion arose because all the gospels say that there was a rush to get his body off the cross and buried before sundown because the "Sabbath" was near. Everyone assumed the reference to "the Sabbath" had to be Saturday so the crucifixion must have been on a

149

Friday. However, as Jews know, the day of Passover itself is also a "Sabbath" or rest day no matter what weekday it falls on. In the year 30 AD Friday, the 15th of the Jewish month Nisan was also a Sabbath so two Sabbaths occurred back to back Friday and Saturday. Matthew seems to know this as he says that the women who visited Jesus' tomb came early Sunday morning "after the Sabbaths" (Matthew 28:1).

As is often the case, the gospel of John preserves a more accurate chronology of what went on. John specifies that the Wednesday night "last supper" was "before the festival of Passover." He also notes that when Jesus' accusers delivered him to be crucified on Thursday morning they would not enter Pilate's courtyard because they would be defiled and would not be able to eat the Passover that evening (John 18:28). John knows that the Jews would be eating their traditional Seder meal Thursday evening.

That discussion sent me checking the plural Sabbaths in Matthew 28:1. It is plural and can be used for either Sabbaths or Sabbath, as also in Matthew 12:1. Most translators opted for singular, but a few retained the literal plural, such as these translations of Matthew 12:1 and 28:1.

At that time Jesus went through the grain on the Sabbath days. And his disciples were hungry and began to pluck the ears of grain and to eat.

New Matthew Bible, © 2016 by Ruth Magnusson (Davis)

At that time did Jesus go on the sabbaths through the corn, and his disciples were hungry, and they began to pluck ears, and to eat,

Young's Literal Translation by Robert Young who compiled Young's Analytical Concordance.

After the Sabbaths, around dawn on the first day of the week, Mary Magdalene and the other Mary went to take a look at the burial site.

International Standard Version, © 1995-2014 by ISV Foundation.

The Bible passages may allow for a crucifixion on the Thursday of Holy Week. Singular or plural, the women found the stone rolled away on the first day of the week after the Sabbath.

That Friday may have been a special Passover Sabbath, not just the Saturday. *Now it was the day of Preparation, and the next day was to be a special Sabbath. Because the Jewish leaders did not want the bodies left on the crosses during the Sabbath, they asked Pilate to have the legs broken and the bodies taken down.* (John 19:31)

Blood Moon AD 31 on Nisan 14

Kevin Woodridge, Ph.D., gives details pointing to a crucifixion date in AD 31 on Thursday, 14th Nisan, including a blood moon on Wednesday night, the beginning of Nisan 14 which continued on Thursday. Friday 15th Nisan, a special Sabbath, was followed by the normal Sabbath on Saturday 16th Nisan, and the resurrection on Sunday 17th Nisan, the first day of the Feast of First Fruits.

His PDF article is **When was Jesus crucified? Evidence pointing to 31 AD**. His Abstract says:

> In which year was Jesus crucified? Many scholars consider that he died sometime between 29 AD and 34

151

AD. A partial lunar eclipse (as described by St. Peter on the Day of Pentecost) on Wednesday 25 April 31 AD (evening/night on the 14th Day of Nisan in the Jewish calendar) corresponds well with the Gospels if the Last Supper were a private "eve of Passover" meal eaten as a Teacher with his disciples one day earlier than others in Jerusalem, followed by Jesus praying and being arrested in the Garden of Gethsemane. The crucifixion of Jesus on Thursday 26 April 31 AD (daytime on the 14th Day of Nisan) corresponds well with the New Testament, if this were followed by a "special Sabbath" for the Passover on the 15th Day of Nisan, then a regular weekly Sabbath on 16th Day of Nisan, then the resurrection of Jesus on 17th Day of Nisan (the First Day of the Feast of First Fruits), with descriptions of fig trees in bloom and bearing "early figs" being suggestive of a late Passover.

He continues:

It is worth noting that the word "Sabbaths" – the Greek word is σαββάτων (sabbaton), which is clearly plural (Nestle et al., 1988) – is used in certain places in the Gospel accounts of the burial and resurrection of Jesus, as shown by Young's Literal Translation:

"And on the eve of the sabbaths, at the dawn, toward the first of the sabbaths, came Mary the Magdalene, and the other Mary, to see the sepulchre." (Matthew 28:1) ...

"And the day was a preparation, and Sabbath was approaching, and the women also who have come with him out of Galilee having followed after, beheld the tomb, and how his body was placed, and having turned back, they made ready spices and ointments, and on the Sabbath, indeed, they rested, according to the command.

And on the first of the <u>sabbaths,</u> at early dawn, they came to the tomb, bearing the spices they made ready, and certain [others] with them, and they found the stone having been rolled away from the tomb, and having gone in, they found not the body of the Lord Jesus." (Luke 23:54-24:3)

"And on the first of the <u>sabbaths,</u> Mary the Magdalene doth come early (there being yet darkness) to the tomb, and she seeth the stone having been taken away out of the tomb, she runneth, therefore, and cometh unto Simon Peter, and unto the other disciple whom Jesus was loving, and saith to them, 'They took away the Lord out of the tomb, and we have not known where they laid him.'" (John 20:1-2)

These two consecutive Sabbaths could have been a "special Sabbath" on the Friday that was the First Day of the Festival of Unleavened Bread (daytime on 15th Day of Nisan), on which no regular or ordinary work was to be done (Leviticus 23:6-7), followed by the regular weekly Sabbath on the Saturday (daytime on 16th Day of Nisan). This *appears* to be borne out by Luke 23:54-24:1, with the women preparing spices and ointments (to anoint the body that had been prepared and buried by Joseph of Arimathea on the Thursday), on the first Sabbath on the Friday, the First Day of the Festival of Unleavened Bread (Figure 3). This was a day on which no regular or ordinary work was to be done, and the preparing of spices and ointments by the women was not "ordinary" work. The next day, the regular weekly Sabbath on the Saturday, the women rested according to the commandment. Then on the Sunday, after the two

Sabbaths, they went to the tomb (Biblical Hermeneutics, 2016). Furthermore, the Gospel of John clearly specifies that the day after Jesus' crucifixion was a "special Sabbath": "Now it was the day of Preparation, and the next day was to be a special Sabbath. Because the Jewish leaders did not want the bodies left on the crosses during the Sabbath, they asked Pilate to have the legs broken and the bodies taken down" (John 19:31). It would have been highly objectionable to the Jewish leaders to allow crucified bodies to remain on the crosses overnight during this special Sabbath (Deuteronomy 21:22-23). All of this indicates that **Jesus was crucified on Thursday 26 April 31 AD (daytime on the 14th Day of Nisan) and was resurrected on Sunday 29 April 31 AD (daytime on the 17th Day of Nisan)**.

Other scholars argue for crucifixion on Wednesday, 25 April, AD 31. See website **Passover Dates 26-34 A.D.**

Many scholars, however, identify the special Passover Sabbath as the Saturday. Some point out that Nisan 14 fell on Friday, April 7 in AD 30, and Friday, April 3 in AD 33, the most likely dates for the crucifixion, based on the dates from the new moon of those years.

Irrespective of the day, the great significance is that the Lamb of God who takes away the sin of the world was crucified on the Day of Preparation for the Passover, the day on which the Passover lamb was killed so that after sunset the Passover could be celebrated on the next Jewish day beginning after sunset.

APPENDIX 5

The Shroud of Turin

The Shroud of Turin is the most intensely investigated religious artifact in history. Many scholars believe it may be the linen cloth that was wrapped around Jesus' body. Its faint image shows the horrendous wounds of a crucified man with wounds exactly matching the description of Jesus' death.

Physicist, and founder of the Shroud of Turin Research Project (STURP), John P. Jackson, has proposed that the image features of the Shroud of Turin were produced by radiation emanating from the body in the Shroud at the moment of resurrection.

> The shroud of Turin is a 14.3 foot by 3.7 linen cloth bearing the faint double image (ventral and dorsal) of a naked man who appears to have been crucified (together with burn marks and water stains resulting from fires, one in 1532).

> There is a puncture wound on his left wrist (his right wrist is hidden from view), and there are puncture wounds on his feet as if they were pierced by a nail or nails. The back of the man is covered with over 120 scourge marks, apparently imposed by the Roman instrument of torture known as the flagrum (a whip with two or three thongs to which were attached small balls of lead). There is a large puncture wound on the right side between the ribs from which blood and a watery serum have flowed. The image resides only on the top-

most fibers of the threads with which the Shroud is woven, and it is a negative image.

Although very faint when viewed as a positive, the image becomes much clearer when darks and lights are reversed.

[Carbon dating in 1988 from a tiny corner of the Shroud dated the sample between 1260 and 1390 AD, but it is argued that the sample came from repaired cloth.]

If the medieval date is right, then this implies that the Shroud is a forgery, when all the scientific evidence we have other than this date implies that it is *not* a forgery: the image on the Shroud was not drawn or painted (there are no binding agents or particulates on the Shroud in the region of the image); it is a negative created at a time when photography didn't exist, but it is not a photograph (it contains 3D information that photographs do not), it is not a contact print (parts of the Shroud that were not in contact with the body bear impressions as clear as parts that were in contact with the body); the man in the Shroud has truly been subject to horrific and mortal injuries; he has wounds associated with crucifixion, and the exit wound on the wrist contradicts depictions of the crucifixion in medieval art, but reflects the way in which people were crucified; he is covered with scourge marks clearly inflicted by the Roman instrument of the torture known as the flagrum, and he has puncture wounds on his head consistent with the wearing of a roughly prepared cap of thorns rather than the elegant wreath of thorns depicted by medieval artists; there is a large wound on his right side which matches a spear used by Roman executioners and from which post-mortem blood and a watery serum (visible only by ultraviolet fluorescence photography) have flowed; the blood on the Shroud – that of a real man – contains a high level of bilirubin, a substance associated with severe physical trauma; there are no signs of decomposition, meaning that the body was removed from the Shroud soon after death; the Shroud contains traces of pollen from plants growing only in the area of Jerusalem, some of which are extinct since antiquity, and there are microscopic traces of dirt at the foot of the man in the Shroud that only match limestone found in the area of Jerusalem.

Source: On the Physics of the Shroud of Turin, 2017, PDF.

See Google for many articles and images from the Shroud of Turin including more details on renewaljournal.com.

Blood trickled from the victim's wrists down his arms, indicating that he hung from his wrists on the cross, not with his arms horizontal as in most crucifixion paintings.

We do not base our faith, or hopes, on an artifact but, although controversial, it does provide confirmation of the brutal torture and trauma of crucifixion that Jesus suffered.

Akiane Kramarik became famous for her paintings and poetry, begun at age four when she started having visions of Jesus and heavenly scenes. An interesting video shows the correlation between the face on the Shroud of Turin and the painting of the vision of Jesus by Akiane: https://www.youtube.com/watch?v=U2AdNTKcGnc

Visions are subjective and open to interpretation, but we live in a time when increasing numbers of people, especially Muslims, are having visions of Jesus that often bring them to trust him as their Saviour and Lord.

APPENDIX 6

Renewal Journal Publications

Logo: basin & towel, lamp & parchment, in the light of the cross

renewaljournal.com

The Renewal Journal website gives links to Renewal Journals, Books, Blogs Free PDFs of all books

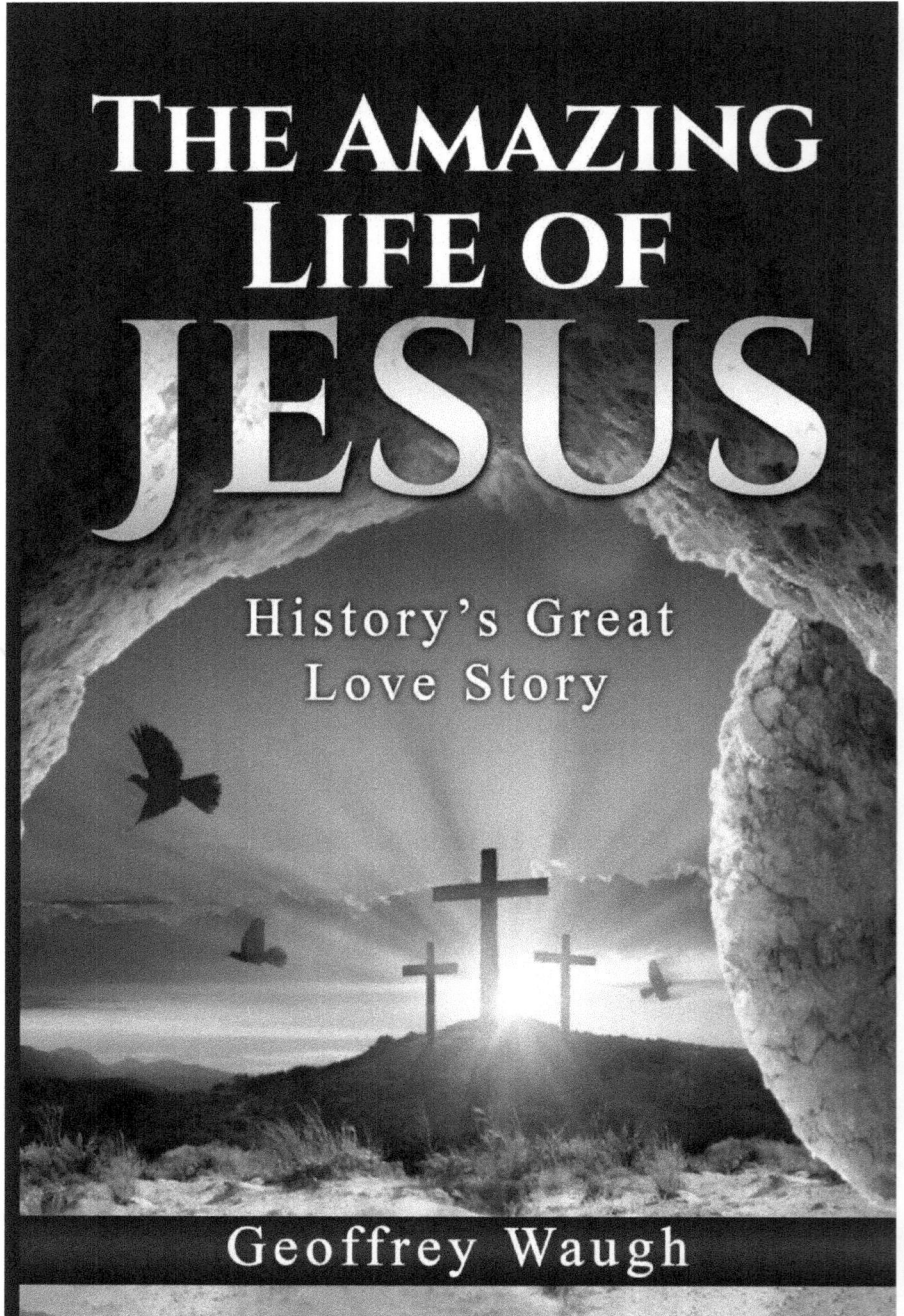

This Renewal Journal version 2024

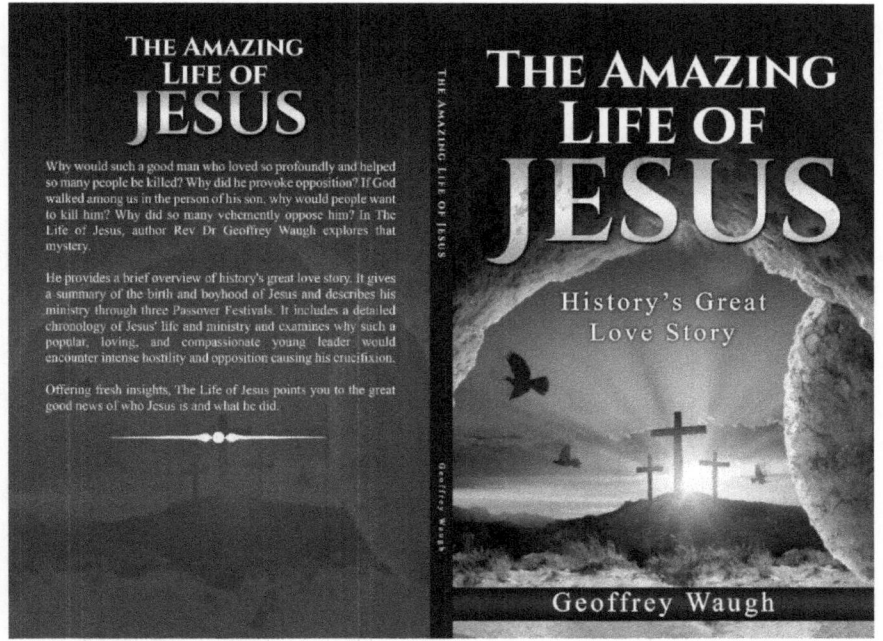

This Renewal Journal version 2024

WestBow Press version 2022

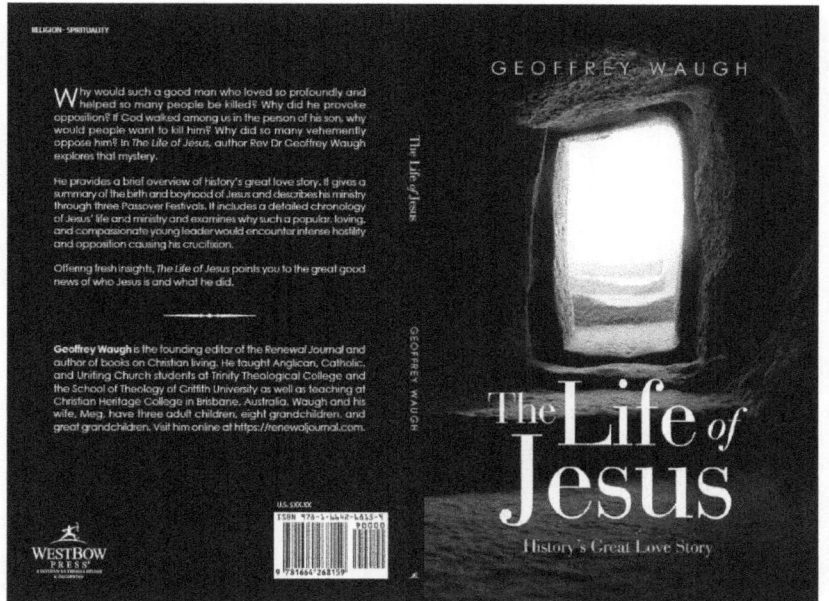

WestBow Press version 2022

Geoff Waugh is the founding editor of the Renewal Journal and the author of publications on Ministry and Mission

The Life of Jesus provides a brief overview of history's great love story. It gives a summary of the birth and boyhood of Jesus and describes his ministry through three Passover Festivals.
The book includes a detailed chart of a chronology of Jesus' life and ministry and examines why such a popular, loving, and compassionate young leader would encounter intense hostility and opposition causing his crucifixion.
The mystery and wonder deepen because his resurrection transformed his followers and millions of lives.
We now date our diaries and calendars from the time of his birth.

The Life of Jesus

The Life of Jesus

History's Great Love Story

Geoff Waugh

First Renewal Journal version 2022
This eBook includes extra imaes

Logo: basin & towel, lamp & parchment, in the light of the cross

www.renewaljournal.com

www.ingramcontent.com/pod-product-compliance
Lightning Source LLC
Chambersburg PA
CBHW041627140626
46547CB00031B/1117